PRAISE FOR *THE INNER MOUNTAIN*

Diane Wang's career journey and commercial success is an inspiration. In her new book, she generously shares her story and offers practical advice on what it takes to build a high-performance career in business and tech. Her life and book will continue to inspire executives around the world to set ambitious goals, be resilient in the face of challenges, and conduct global commerce with purpose.

— **Katherine Rich**
Interim Chief Executive, Aged Care Association NZ (ACA)

Diane Wang's 'The Inner Mountain' is a transformative guide to self-discovery, blending ancient wisdom with modern insights from her pioneering career in cross-border e-commerce. As founder of The Inner Mountain Foundation and a champion for women's development globally, Wang's book offers readers a roadmap to navigate life's peaks and valleys and unlock their full potential.

— **Silvana Koch-Mehrin**
Founder & President, Women Political Leaders

Diane Wang not only embodies the essence of leadership by providing direction, purpose, and wisdom but also adeptly integrates insights on digitalisation into today's business landscape. Her guidance in The Inner Mountain is timely and invaluable, offering a roadmap for navigating the post-pandemic challenges and leading teams to new heights. Whether managing a small startup or a large organisation, Diane offers essential and personal advice that resonates with leaders striving to thrive amidst change.

— John Denton
Secretary General, International Chamber of Commerce (ICC)

THE INNER
MOUNTAIN

THE INNER MOUNTAIN

DISCOVER YOUR TRUE
SPIRIT, STRENGTH, AND POTENTIAL

DIANE WANG

FOUNDER, CHAIRPERSON, & CEO OF DHGATE
AUTHOR, SPEAKER, ENTREPRENEUR

2022 & 2023 BUSINESS WOMAN OF THE YEAR
(CEO TODAY MAGAZINE)

Forbes | Books

Published by Forbes Books, Charleston, South Carolina.
An imprint of Advantage Media Group.

Forbes Books is a registered trademark, and the Forbes Books colophon is a trademark of Forbes Media, LLC.

Printed in the United States of America.

10 9 8 7 6 5 4 3 2 1

ISBN: 979-8-88750-104-8 (Hardcover)
ISBN: 979-8-88750-105-5 (eBook)

Library of Congress Control Number: 2024905936

Cover design by Lance Buckley.
Layout design by Ruthie Wood.

This custom publication is intended to provide accurate information and the opinions of the author in regard to the subject matter covered. It is sold with the understanding that the publisher, Forbes Books, is not engaged in rendering legal, financial, or professional services of any kind. If legal advice or other expert assistance is required, the reader is advised to seek the services of a competent professional.

Since 1917, Forbes has remained steadfast in its mission to serve as the defining voice of entrepreneurial capitalism. Forbes Books, launched in 2016 through a partnership with Advantage Media, furthers that aim by helping business and thought leaders bring their stories, passion, and knowledge to the forefront in custom books. Opinions expressed by Forbes Books authors are their own. To be considered for publication, please visit **books.Forbes.com**.

To my husband, Jun,

my parents,

my kids, Hui-Hui, Bu-Bu

CONTENTS

INTRODUCTION 1
What Is the Inner Mountain?

CHAPTER 1 7
Talk to Your Heart

CHAPTER 2 23
The Digital World Can Change Your Career

CHAPTER 3 47
We Can't Win If We Fight the Wrong Battle

CHAPTER 4 65
Reframing the Narrow Definition of Success

CHAPTER 5 83
Dare to Fail; Dare to Do

CHAPTER 6 95
From Intuition to Self-Love

CHAPTER 7 111
Wolf and Water

CHAPTER 8 119
Looking to the Future

CONTACT IMF 127

ACKNOWLEDGMENTS 129

ABOUT THE AUTHOR 133

INTRODUCTION

What Is the Inner Mountain?

In many ways, the book you are holding is the book I wish I had when I started. It's the message I deliver when I mentor women, and I hope that it speaks to you, that it informs you, and that it inspires you to take the next step—and the next.

The Inner Mountain

Do you have those moments when you're engrossed in work all day? You come home late at night and feel exhausted? Do you tell yourself it will get better? That you just need to keep pushing ahead?

No matter how successful you are at work or how great your achievements are, there will always be those moments of frustration and lack of fulfillment. Because you are eager for more and want to be better, you're probably already starting to realize that this road will never end. You are not alone. Many share the same experiences and feelings. And so have I.

Perhaps you have found yourself in a situation similar to where I was when I began my career. You're successful by everyone else's definition. The people you care for are proud of you, and yet, there is something missing, something you can't quite define. That something begins to gnaw at you; it's like a tiny voice whispering, "There's more. There's more." You can ignore the voice and distract yourself with other pursuits. Indeed, you might even bury yourself in your current position, telling yourself it's enough and that you should be grateful to be where you are. I suggest you look within. You might think of this as intuition, which is both rational and emotional; I call it talking to your heart. It's a moment of intuitive thinking without logical analysis and too much calculation.

When I started writing this book, it was for two reasons: I wanted to speak out, and I wanted to serve others. I realized that I had been limited by my preconceived notion that "less talk, more action" was a virtue. I further realized that this self-limiting belief has influenced me for ten years. I used to fully unleash my courage to think and do; however, I have not spoken up. I'm aware that what inspires and motivates my mission and vision can also inspire and motivate others.

What I learned

Life is like climbing a mountain filled with uncertainties. The first mountain for most of us is like the drive for success, focused around reaching the summit of professional and worldly success, a job, a profession, wealth, and status. I felt that drive, and I climbed that mountain. At first, you climb that first mountain because you do want to be successful. You learn how to do this. You succeed at doing this. Sometimes it takes a while, but you will climb and conquer it.

But what happens then? You have climbed this mountain, but then you realize there are higher peaks to conquer. It's as if you are playing an endless game, and you are always dealing with anxiety and the ever-present drain of competition. What if you turn away from the mountain and turn within? That is what this book will encourage you to do. To turn to your inner mountain.

If more of us discover our inner motivation, we can start to enlighten those around us. That is also a goal of my book, to reach outside my life and my business.

What this book isn't

It's not a blueprint. It's a guide.

It's not a pep talk about how successful you must be. Success is a personal, possibly spiritual matter.

What this book is

It's the encouragement I wish I could share with more people personally. It's the confirmation to the thoughts you might already be having about a need for something more in your life.

Discovering our inner mountain is a journey. It's something I found only after my journey in the business world. I'm learning even more about it now as founder of the Inner Mountain Foundation, which I'll describe shortly. I liken the journey to what the NASA astronauts experienced; an astronaut while flying to the moon captured images of the lunar surface. Then he unintentionally turned his camera and, at that moment, saw and captured the Earth from a different perspective. I don't think anyone spoke as they saw the Earth from such a different viewpoint. Once we have experienced a moment like that, we are led to profound change. Ultimately, armed with this different perspective, we find our calling.

When we are that profoundly changed, we are not the same person anymore. That's what happened to me when I discovered my inner mountain. Now, I'm focused on both speaking *and* doing. Through the Inner Mountain Foundation, we have outlined an achievable blueprint for how to fulfill our initial mission and vision. For me, this is also a motivation. Similar to the astronaut described earlier, I hope to have a reflection that helps me discover a new perspective. I believe others will do the same, and I hope you will be one of them. My goal is to help you experience an inner journey that will lead you to see that the world is not only what you have previously seen and that there is so much more to discover.

So where do you begin? I believe by talking to your heart.

CHAPTER 1

Talk to Your Heart

It is only with the heart that one can see rightly. What is essential is invisible to the eye.

—Antoine de Saint-Exupéry, *The Little Prince*

Sometimes, when I explain to someone that I talk to my heart to find direction, I receive a questioning look or even an indulgent smile in return. Yet, this seemingly simple practice has served me well in building a career even when I was uncertain about my path. I need to point out that I don't do this only as I'm coming up with a concept for a project or a pivot. I do it at various steps in the process. In other words, although I rely on research, a strong team, and my past experience, I don't rely on them alone. If I did, I might be continuing on my path of business success only, and business success is not enough. I think it's important to connect with the energy of your heart. When

I do this, I'm able to tap into my inner strength, and I feel powerful at the core.

While understanding and honoring that everyone has a different way of connecting with their heart, I'm going to show you how doing so has worked for me. That means that in this chapter, I, who prefer to look ahead, am going to look back.

From the natural world, to Tsinghua University, the beginning

The experience of country life gave me an independent personality and the courage to persevere. I was born in Beijing, but when I was about seven years old, it happened that I had my grade one school term between 1976 and 1977 in the rural area of Hebei, a northern province of China.

Diane in school

I spent about one hour walking to my school every day. On my way there, I went through farmlands and had to climb over ditches and ridges, as well as pass through a swampy area with wild dogs—all this while carrying a chair and a schoolbag. Strange as it may sound, at that time, there was no fixed place for our school and classrooms. We needed to find a classroom by ourselves before the class. Sometimes, we hung the blackboard in the woods or close to a haystack, while at other times, we were fortunate to find an empty room.

What impressed me deeply was not the difficult learning environment and challenging school conditions but the flat land, extending all the way to the horizon. Looking back, I would say that was a time that my mind was closest to the nature. From the bottom of my heart, I felt that I could do whatever I wanted to do in those rural farmlands.

Nature itself represents power. It inspires us to be real, to be open, to be strong.

Even as that young girl coming from the big city to the country, I needed to be a fighter to survive. It was a matter of self-defense and defending my peers, especially those who were more timid and vulnerable than me. When you are the city kid coming to a new school, you are the underdog, and the bullies won't go away unless you force them to. I stood up to the boys who were taller and stronger than I was, and I defeated them.

I didn't even know I had bravery in my heart. I simply reacted as my true self when I was threatened. In one encounter, I grabbed the bully by his collar and pushed him down the slope. I protected myself when my mother wasn't around. As a result, I often listened to my inner voice and made my own decisions. I had no choice, and those early habits served me well when I was older. I no longer had to fight grade-school bullies, but I did need to stand up for myself and to remind myself, even in difficult situations, that I was a fighter.

Of course, by the time I got to middle school, I was too small to fight back physically, but I was always strong in my attitude and beliefs, and I grew even stronger along the way.

I believe it's easier to open your heart and connect yourself with nature at a young age because you are naïve, and what you think intuitively has little interference from prejudice and stereotype. When people ask me how you can learn the ability to talk to your heart, I tell them that everyone has their own way. For example, I had a unique "self" moment when I experienced being under a sky full of stars on a Dunhuang desert trip. Others may feel that moment when walking alone in the middle of nowhere. There's no standard formula. Since childhood, I also kept a diary, which is another way of communicating with yourself. By the time I reached university, I had developed the habit of asking myself fundamental questions and, just as important, acting on the answers.

My first job was at Tsinghua University, which is one of the top two universities in China. This was a good job that satisfied my parents' hopes for me because they both worked at a university too. Even though my family and friends valued the stability and prestige of the university job, I yearned for something more fulfilling, and my inner voice gave me the courage to pursue what I thought might be better for me.

Diane at Tsinghua University

The workload was not so heavy. In fact, it was so light that I could complete the entire week's work on Monday. Then I would sit in on some university lectures from the history or other departments the rest of the week.

There was something else going on as well. I was concerned about the future. At the moment, I was pretty relaxed in my position, but I didn't know what might lie ahead. Even then, I knew I would rather face hard and even challenging work; I wanted something to open up my mind.

I began to ask myself, "*Is this what you want?*" The answer was that this wasn't all I wanted. I craved more challenge, more work. I wanted and needed something that would excite me when I rose every morning, something that would, even in the face of obstacles, keep me moving ahead, energized, and committed.

I think this is a good example of talking to my heart and taking action to follow my inner voice intuitively. When you listen to your heart, and you hear the answer, there is a next step. You take action. That is what I did. I began to seek out opportunities. And when you seek, you find.

Microsoft, the first big challenge

It was a very early stage in China for multinational companies. We were just starting to become aware of Microsoft and AT&T. Our generation was lucky. We experienced the booming period for the IT industry from the early to late 1990s. And then, from 2000 onward, we also experienced the booming stage of the internet sector in China. Even though I didn't know much about Microsoft, something about it appealed to me. It was a new and challenging world. I am not fond of calm lakes. I enjoy charging through rapids. And to me, at that time, Microsoft offered the most challenging rapids.

My need to change didn't make sense to some of my friends, and I know my parents were concerned. Certainly, my mum didn't want me to deal with stress at work and was hoping I'd be satisfied with a job that gave me more time to enjoy life. However, working hard and taking risks are my life, and I was already restless, even though I wasn't sure of the path I would take.

In time, I realized that different people have different characteristics. I'm very clear about which type I am. I like to challenge myself and keep trying new things. I think of it like this: I want to do things that make my eyes shine. Although my parents worried about me, I was persistent in going in the direction I chose.

While I was determined to try something new, there were almost no openings for me back in 1992, which was also the year China started to pivot from a planned economy to a market economy. I had just over a year's working experience at a university, but I had no plan to move from one university to another while the private sector economy was yet to boom.

Luckily, Microsoft entered the Chinese mainland in 1992, posting recruitment advertisements on newspapers. Secretary to the general manager was the only position I thought might fit me, so I applied. I got the interview, waited for a long time, but received no notice at all. I knew I had probably been rejected. I could face up to the reality silently, stay at my position at the university, or simply move on to search for different opportunities. After fierce internal struggles, I decided to take one more step to know why Microsoft didn't want to hire me. So, I phoned.

"You're not a fit for that position," the manager told me. That was disappointing; I really wanted to work for the company. "But," he said, "we do have an opening in the marketing department."

New environment, new culture

I joined Microsoft in 1993, the second year it entered China. I wish I could say it was an easy transition. A university is far different from a private company, and I experienced culture shock as I learned my new job. I had left the cloistered world of the university and put myself in this entirely different environment that was new to me and new to China. Everything felt so cold, and I longed for the warmth of my former job. For the first three days, I wanted to quit. For the first week, I wanted to quit. After I survived the first three months, I celebrated.

I really appreciate Microsoft and the opportunities that position provided me. Of course, as a female in the company, I had to prove myself maybe three or four times more than my male counterparts if I hoped to be promoted. I also realized that along with the totally different methodology and mindset of running a company, there was a lack of cordiality. Chinese society values *mianzi* and tends to avoid conflicts. Let's just say that my new colleagues did not value *mianzi*.

In my position at the university, we all treated one another like family members. We were cordial, and we tried to be polite to one another. Working for a multinational company in the 1990s varied greatly from what I had known. Most people focused on individual excellence. As a rule, they didn't care about teamwork or friendship as much as they cared about results. At Microsoft, in the early stage of my employment, they told me, "When you do a presentation, if you bullshit, people will throw tomatoes and eggs at your face." That shocked me.

A FIGHTER

Despite the challenges, I did not want to give up. Yes, it was different from working for the university, where we tried to get along even when we disagreed, but I wanted to succeed. Part of that is the fighter side of my personality.

I experienced culture shock in the workplace, yet I chose to take a more positive approach. I told myself I was making progress even when I was struggling. Time and again, I would be passed over for a promotion, and I would try to see the strengths of the new manager; I would try not to be angry. The story repeated itself my first few years at Microsoft.

I was adaptable; I had to be. That adaptability was another trait that helped me at Microsoft. I became known as the person who would get it done, regardless of what "it" was. The phrase "to carry a message to Garcia," harkening back to an 1899 true story, is used to describe someone taking an initiative when carrying out a difficult assignment. You have to be quick, and you have to be effective. I worked hard to be that person who could always be counted on. My philosophy at this time was this: If you cannot change the situation, if it is out of your control, then do something you *can* control. If you take a negative or a victimized attitude, you hurt no one but yourself.

PAVING FOR THE FUTURE

The several areas Microsoft allowed me to explore also paved the way for my future. First was the global perspective. This was the first time I was able to travel abroad and attend global events. I visited the company headquarters and worked with people around the world. As a result, I became gradually better acquainted and familiar with the culture. That experience of doing business in the global market, not only in the Chinese market, would stay with me and fuel my later dreams.

Microsoft also gave me an opportunity to explore the freedom, innovation, and openness of the company. The values of striving to win and to become number one in the market became my own values as well, and they stayed with me even after I left Microsoft.

LEAVING MICROSOFT

At this time, Microsoft was the most successful company in the world. I could only see a little part of the company, and the company itself was only part of the business world; I longed to leave and see the outside world. I was like the proverbial frog in the well. I could see only a small part of the sky. Only after I left the well could I see how big and wonderful the world really is.

I was Microsoft's youngest department manager ever in Mainland China. So when people heard I was about to leave, no one could understand why. By now, you might have an idea of why I chose that path.

Diane at Microsoft

I had been with Microsoft for six years, and along with my colleagues, I began hearing a lot of talk about the internet. I knew little about the internet industry, and I was intrigued much in the same way I had been intrigued by the world outside my university job. As I had then, I decided to march into the unknown because I wanted to learn and do new things. My intuition told me that "the internet is the future" and that I needed to get into this industry and ride with it.

What does a pioneer in the internet sector look like? That was the question I asked myself. That question would lead me to the next step in my career.

I joined Cisco Systems.

Dream high, work hard

At Cisco, I was the only female senior executive on the company management team. Yet, again, I looked beyond what I was doing to what I might accomplish, and the answer from my heart was clear. This next step had to be something I did on my own. I wanted my own business in the internet industry. I just needed to find the right one and make my move. I mentioned before in this chapter that I was always looking for something to make my eyes shine, and nothing made them shine more than the thought of having my own business.

What drove me to be bold enough to quit the promising, uprising position in Fortune 500 companies and leave for an unknown entre-preneurial journey? It's not only because I spotted an opportunity; it's also because I listened to what was coming from such a driving force in my heart. This was my inner voice, and I was determined that this would be my next goal, my next mountain. At that time, I was also questioning my own power. When you work for a major company, it's much easier for you to negotiate with different partners. So you might feel that you are so strong, you are so successful, you are so capable. Whenever you talk to others, they say, "Oh yes, I want to work with you." It's easy to translate that into a false sense of importance.

I asked myself this question: *Do they want to work with me because of the glory of the company, or is it because of my capabilities?* When you work for one of the world's most successful companies, you can negotiate, and you can succeed. *But is that because of you or because of the company that employs you?* Once I asked myself that question, I could not ignore the answer.

At that time, Cisco was the most popular internet company in the industry. I was still a young woman, and I needed to—I had to—find out who I was. I wanted to see if my creativity and my ideas were as good as I felt they were, not because of the company but because of me. If I were wrong, if I failed after leaving the company, I would accept it. But I needed to—I had to—try.

WHY LEAVE?

I had the creativity, and I wanted the freedom, to try out new ideas. It was similar to the way I felt when I left the university job. I could face failure, but I couldn't restrict myself from being all that I could be.

These jobs, regardless of the challenges, confined my creativity. I had to follow guidelines from headquarters and postpone my initiatives to be more productive and successful. Following instructions from headquarters located thousands of miles away frustrated me. I was in the battlefield. I was the one who spotted opportunities and carried out solutions according to the real-time market changes. If you hear these messages in your head, perhaps you are the same way:

I'm innovative. I'm creative. I want to be unique.
I want to see my creativity become a reality.
I want to realize my potential. I want to be a pioneer.

At the time, no one really knew what the internet meant or where it would go, if it would go anywhere at all. Entrepreneurship in the internet sector had great challenges, and we weren't sure what they were. I did know the business I was contemplating would require a lot of imagination. Still, I didn't have clear ideas about what I would encounter in those early days of the start-up business. That didn't matter. I might not have had all the answers, but I had inspiration.

Leaving Cisco to start my first business, Joyo.com, was the time when I received the strongest opposition from the people in my life. They simply could not understand why I would give up everything I had accomplished for an unproven dream. There was a positive side to their doubts, however. After that, no matter what wild things I did, no one close to me was shocked. In their minds, if I would leave two major companies, if I would step out on my own in an unknown industry, I was capable of anything.

When I started Joyo.com, no one supported my decision, but it didn't really matter because I followed my true calling: I made that decision based on my inner explorer, and I encountered no struggle at all. Of course, nobody was sure if the decision was the right one, but I was 100 percent ready to take on the challenge and face tough situations, including, if need be, failure.

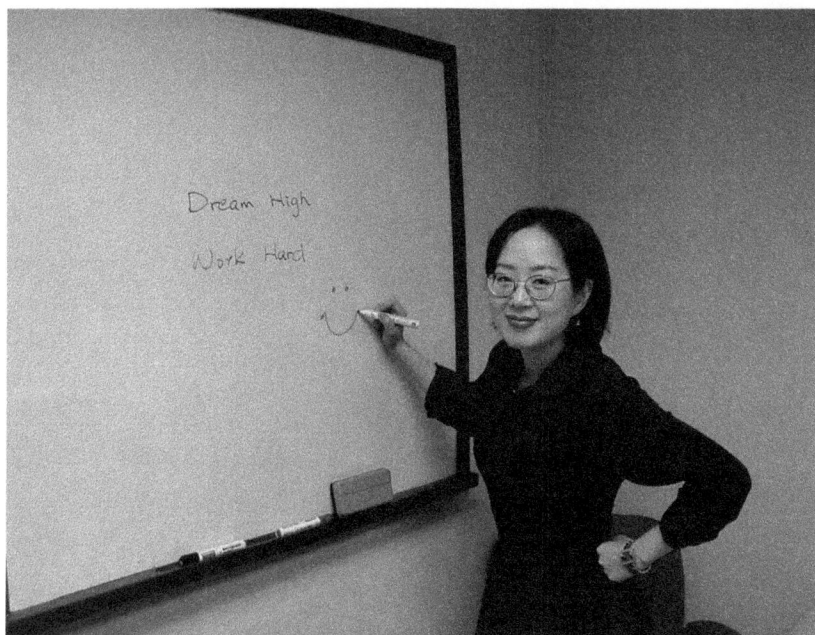

Diane leaving Cisco to start her venture

I wanted to see who I am. I was only twenty-nine years old, and I could accept failures. I remember my last day at Cisco was a freezing-cold day at the end of 1999. I left this parting message on my whiteboard: "Dream high, work hard." And my husband took a picture of it. And then, I closed the door and said goodbye to the first steps of my journey in the workplace, with high expectations for the future, not knowing I was to "dance on the edge of a sword." This is also the photo that I looked at from time to time, reminding me of where my new journey had started.

Sometimes, there is too much noise surrounding you, and you're also dealing with expectations—other people's and society's. We are so busy trying to figure out things in our minds that we forget how to listen to our hearts.

Your body doesn't lie. Listen to the sensation of your body, and try to do something the inner you is passionate about. It is the most important part of starting a business and probably an essential part of living your best life. History can also be a source of energy and wisdom. As I will say more than once in this book, we are all connected to one another. We are also connected to the people and the events that came before us.

> ### Reflection exercise
>
> • When have you listened to your heart? When did you first know that you could trust your inner voice?
> • What dreams do you have about where you want to go next?
> • What obstacles do you have?

Next

In the past, and especially in certain cultures, there were only so many ways a woman could succeed in business. Now, thanks to the digital world, all of that has changed.

CHAPTER 2

The Digital World Can Change Your Career

I hate to hear you talk about all women as if they were fine ladies instead of rational creatures. None of us want to be in calm waters all our lives.

—Jane Austen, Persuasion

When you feel driven to do something, regardless of the odds, you need to follow what your heart tells you if only because you will need your inner fortitude to keep you going through the rough times. And there will be rough times.

I had left not one secure job but three, and I was convinced that, regardless of the outcome, I would not regret my decision. E-commerce made my transition possible, and as I look both back and around, I see that it has done that for other women as well.

Joyo.com

As I look back, I see a consistency in my actions. I was creative, and my jobs confined my creativity. Guidelines from headquarters postponed my initiatives that I believed would lead us to being more productive and successful. I was excited by the thought of the freedom to try out new ideas. I could face failure, but I wouldn't restrict myself from reaching my full potential.

So, yes, there is consistency here, the consistency of wanting to achieve more and make the world different.

When I was young, I didn't realize that this consistency was my "formula," a part of who I am. Start-ups fail easily, so I had a significant number of uncertainties; however, I have the heart for that. I'm not afraid.

Now I believe that the character of a person determines the action, and the action determines the fate.

DOUBTS AND DETERMINATION

As I shared in the last chapter, I made the jump to a company of my own despite concerns from those who care about me. I did it because I believed I could be more and achieve more. At the end of 1999, as one of the first generation of e-commerce entrepreneurs in China, I co-founded Joyo.com, an online book and video retailer, and the first B2C e-commerce platform there.

Diane at Joyo.com

In the early days, I had to struggle to find my direction. During the first three months, my team and I had fierce debates about where we were headed and what we really wanted to do. The so-called internet industry was new, and we were rookies. It was as if we had been put in a dense forest, and we had to find our way out. The company's development direction took a considerable amount of time for debate on what exactly to pursue in the realm of the internet. We explored numerous possibilities, including portals, gaming, travel, and e-commerce. These directions had significant distinctions, and determining our path was a crucial decision. For days and weeks, we engaged in intense discussions, debating the pros and cons of various possibilities day and night. The conversations seemed endless, and a decision remained elusive along that path. At that moment, having clarity about what you wanted was essential in making such a decision. In the end, I slammed my hand on the desk and declared, "That's it.

We're going this way." Eventually, the choice was made to venture into e-commerce. This was a pivotal moment. The decision was finalized by the end of February 2000.

Then, Nasdaq collapsed, and along with it, hope. There was no so-called strategy or planning tactics.

At that time, we were like abandoned orphans. Investors had no hope for us, considering their investment as good as gone. They saw us as wavering, burning through money, and they didn't expect us to survive. Even our employees were pessimistic. Despite this lack of confidence, we bravely held a press conference. I still remember the pitying expressions of the journalists at that event. The only thing that might get us through, I knew, was a leader who had the willingness to continue the battle. I resolved to remain composed and stand firm.

We launched our website in May, and many thought we were finished before we started. I remember the expressions on the faces of some of the journalists in my office right before I went into the press conference room. They looked at me with pity. In my heart, I also felt that maybe we were reckless and wrong and that maybe the bad timing would destroy us. But I still needed to go to that conference room to stand on the stage and launch our website.

Everyone competing at that time had a different idea about what approach would get us where we needed to go. It was like climbing mountains. We didn't know which path would lead to survival. So, in the very beginning, we had four groups of people climbing the mountain together. The other three hit the dead end. And only one team survived.

Some companies went from being well-funded to financially strained, or their strategies started wavering. At that time, our approach was highly pragmatic, eschewing flashy packaging. This pragmatic stance helped us survive.

Navigating through these darkest moments and emerging from them meant we could stand out like a dark horse. Through jungles, swamps, and deserted islands, it became possible to find direction. Those were exciting times. We couldn't wait to check the sales at midnight when one day ended. Sometimes, we worked until three o'clock in the morning.

ANOTHER TRANSITION

Early in China's internet history, we didn't have much venture capital. I knew the fate of the company, and that was that sooner or later, we would be sold. It wasn't something I could control. Although I hadn't wanted to build a company just to sell it, I knew if I stayed longer, maybe I would waste more time. So, two and a half years into that first start-up, I chose to quit.

I also had another mission I needed to fulfill. I wanted to have my first baby.

Joyo was acquired by Amazon in 2004 and renamed Amazon China. And at age thirty-five, I gave birth to my daughter.

DHgate: Disruptive innovation

For a long time, I thought about the next thing that would "make my eyes shine." What would it be? I had been doing ToC business in the Chinese market for a long time, so I was very much looking forward to doing something different. I thought the B2B international market was the direction, and I knew e-commerce would be part of that.

When I founded DHgate, I developed my idea based on three keywords: internet, international, and MSMEs (Micro, Small, and Medium Enterprises). These three keywords finished my puzzle at the time. I believe e-commerce can empower MSMEs, which can create a more enormous impact than consumer business.

Starting at DHgate

And based on these three words, we worked out a whole new world in DHgate.

At that time, there were no exports completed in the form of e-commerce. Traditional online information service was more like an online version of the yellow pages. The path was uncharted, and chances of survival were uncertain. I took a chance to create a business model that went far beyond that. I knew that setting it up would take tremendous time and energy; it would be a marathon, not a sprint, assuming we could make it work and that the model we envisioned was even possible. But I also believed that once the platform was established, we'd have countless opportunities for growth, if we survived.

DHgate's business model is one of disruptive innovation because we came up with a brand-new concept. We believed that what we were doing was not only a global trade that goes (slightly) digital but also a digitalized global trade. We would help MSMEs achieve online transactions with global buyers from all over the world. In short, I visualized DHgate as a new model to connect buyers and sellers, enabling them to complete international transactions online.

In the past, Alibaba ran only an online yellow-page model, allowing suppliers to upload pictures and descriptions about their product. And now, we intended to integrate the whole package of services, including logistics, payment, and customer relationship management, into an online platform. That way, buyers could complete international procurement with a simple click.

Imagine a scenario where everyone believes the Earth is square, not round. Yet, you firmly believe it's round. So, you embark on a solo voyage, and though many perish in the sea, you remain undeterred, steadfast in your dream. That was my journey. I knew we could eventually come full circle.

OUR NAME AND OUR MISSION

When you name a company, as I did DHgate Group, it's important to think about what that name stands for in the market, but also I believe, what it means to you personally. DH stands for Dunhuang, which is located in northwest China on the ancient Silk Road. It used to be the most important international trading center in ancient China, a gateway where exported products, as well as ancient Chinese civilization, traveled from China to other countries and vice versa. At one time, Dunhuang was one of the ancient world's most important intersections between the East and the West, where the ancient Chinese, Indian, Greek, and Persian civilizations met and merged.

Early DHgate staff gathering

I came up with the name for our company in a small café in 2004 when I was just starting. This name means the blending of Eastern and Western cultures and the drive to create and make new things. I drew the idea on a napkin. I thought about our goal, which was to create a disruptive, innovative, cross-border e-commerce platform, enabling suppliers in one country and buyers in another country to make a deal and finish the transactions online. Dunhuang, the most important international trading center in ancient China, came to my mind. It was not only that the prosperity of trade appealed to me, but I was also struck by the fact that, within this context, there are diverse cultures, including religion, blending and benefiting from one another. This kind of fusion and inheritance requires both material and spiritual aspects, and that appealed to me as well. It represents the values we aspire to: solidarity, practicality, and creativity. I saw it as a fusion of the East and the West. "DH" is actually derived from the East. It's an English term, and from the start, I desired this kind of fusion. So it's an East–West communication and integration. It holds our cultural values. We can think big, create, and innovate.

Prosperity of ancient markets

Yes, I thought. We will build a modern Silk Road online. And with that goal, DHgate was born.

The difference was that, in ancient times, cross-border commerce was through camel transportation. Today, we use the internet for cross-border e-commerce. And, of course, we were not only about trading goods, but we were also at the forefront of the interaction of different ideas and cultures from all over the world.

As I thought about how well this name fit our company, I remembered that, in ancient times, people embarked on a road from Dunhuang to other countries or came to Dunhuang from the West, all of them on a long journey full of uncertainty and risks. Although they came from different cultures, the inner strengths of bravery, persistence, daring to explore, openness, and kindness were the same. I did and still believe that DHgate shares the exact origin and the values of ancient Dunhuang handed down over thousands of years.

Trip to Dunhuang

This was a totally new business model, so we couldn't continue the existing terms in the market, such as "Made-in-China" and "Trade-on-line," despite how easily recognized they were. My unchanged belief over the past twenty years is that DHgate, as the first mover in cross-border e-commerce, stands for a spirit of Chinese and Western integration. Our mission was to promote global trade and to support entrepreneurial dreams, and our vision was and is to empower everyone in the global trade.

We are always thinking how to bridge more, how to understand and appreciate different cultures more, to help more MSMEs, and we still aim to achieve more in this direction.

Our name also applies to the visual and logo design of DHgate. com. "DH" is in boldface black and gray, which represents the stability of the company. "Gate" is in gold, with creative world art, symbolizing innovation, vitality, and energy. After twenty years, I feel as if we're sailing a boat. In times of easy seas and times of storm, we never change. At the same time, we continue to strive for cutting-edge innovation in the market.

THE WIN-OR-GO-HOME MOMENT

Before DHgate.com went online, most investors were reluctant because they wanted data to prove my idea was workable. Of course, we had no data and would not until the website went online. From 2004 to 2005, I met with dozens of investors. One investor in Shenzhen negotiated an investment of USD $3 or $4 million. So, we recruited nearly fifty people. The term sheet was signed. When it came to the payment due date, I heard nothing from them, so I called the investor. He either didn't answer or just avoided talking about the issue. This investment was going to be a lifesaver for us. The platform was waiting to go online, and without the investment, we would have no money to pay employee salaries the next month. I immediately bought a plane ticket to Shenzhen and went directly to the investor.

He sat behind his ancient Chinese mahogany table, and the very air in his house felt gloomy. I had already invested several million yuan in my company, and more importantly, the platform was about to go live.

"What's wrong?" I asked the investor.

"I decided not to invest."

"But we already signed a contract," I said. "If we have no money, we'll have to shut down the company."

I can still remember the expression of finality on his face as he said, "I'm sorry. That's it."

It was raining that day and freezing cold. The outside weather matched my inside, hopeless with no sign of warmth or reprieve. In the plane returning to Beijing, I just wanted to fly forever and not land because I didn't know how to fix a company with no revenue, a company only I seemed to believe in.

But the plane landed anyway, and I knew I had to go to my office and face all the problems. We were counting on that investment in February or March, and we launched the website in May. I didn't know how to face my colleagues, and the company's remaining funds were only enough to sustain the expenses of fewer than ten employees. I had long heard the expression about rats deserting a sinking ship, but my ship hadn't even set sail yet. *It might be a small boat*, I thought, *but it is still a boat, and even if we are thrown off the boat, perhaps, there is a small board to cling to.* Not only were potential investors wary about my ideas, but so were many of the people I hired, as well. As a result, many of those people from the foreign trade sector left. A company vice president told me the day he left, "I quite understand your decision, even though I think your idea is quite unreliable. It's good to have this kind of dream if it can be realized."

I had no choice but to spend my own money to pay the remaining employees. The last straw was gone, and every day after that was like walking on the edge of a knife. When we almost ran out of money, we surrendered the office and moved to a twenty-square-meter conference room next to the toilet of a friend's company. It was empty because no one else wanted it. At Microsoft and Cisco, I'd been an executive with my own office. Now, my remaining staff and I were practically sitting on top of one another. My office chair was broken, but my hope was strong. That shaky broken chair felt like my raft.

We're fortunate, I thought. We had one another, and we had our shared hope. Even though I was failing, I could still hold on to a small plank and breathe.

Then one day in June, my colleague Richard shouted something that would change my life forever. "Wow, we just got our first order!" $6.14 for a laptop bag. We celebrated as if it were a million because it was the sign we had been waiting for, the sign that we were on the right track.

By the end of 2005, we had achieved nearly USD $1 million a year. The numbers increased month after month. In December 2005, I met Tina, the investor of TDF Capital, who understood what I was talking about. Yes, we were able to leave that office, yet I still remember that broken chair fondly. It didn't let me down, and together, we made it through the doubts, the disappointments, and the rough times.

Most entrepreneurs have experienced that kind of win-or-go-home moment, but very few have survived. An entrepreneur must be more resilient to unexpected challenges. When facing a challenge, most people would see 99.9 percent of the problems and difficulties. Only true entrepreneurs see 0.1 percent of possibility and opportunity. I am the one who focuses on the 0.1 percent, and I do my best to make it a reality.

By 2008, the company that investors had turned their backs on was listed seventh on the Deloitte Technology Fast 50 for the Asia-Pacific region. By 2009, it had one million registered buyers.

The culture of DHgate also reflects my values of practicality and innovation. At the end of 1999, during the first wave of China's internet boom, many professional managers left multinationals to join the entrepreneurial journey, but 99 percent of them failed when trying to establish a business. One critical element—practicality—got us through the hard times. In multinationals, subsidiary managers don't need to worry about the headquarter strategy, and they have numerous resources at hand, without worrying about survival. However, this isn't the case for entrepreneurs. By necessity, their mindset differs from the 0-to-1 kind of start-up mindset.

On the one hand, I like to think "big." I believe we can change the world (because we can). On the other hand, I value practicality.

I'm proud that DHgate took the first steps to digital trade. Yes, we were disruptive. Most people could not understand what we were going to do at the time because no one had done it. DHgate was a game changer. We paved the way for the current cross-border e-commerce industry and formulated the initial industry standards from scratch.

MYYSHOP BORN ON THE FOUNDATION OF DHGATE

While DHgate, as a centralized marketplace, was developing on the right path for years, social platforms like Facebook and Instagram and the most recent and ubiquitous one—TikTok—are taking center stage in our lives.

A large mass of individuals, especially Generation Z, like to generate content on such platforms, influencing their followers, and some even attempt to lure them to buy products by offering detailed information, often in the form of videos or live streams—a drastic change from text and still images on a traditional e-commerce website.

In 2021, anticipating the boom of social commerce, which marks the decentralization of e-commerce, and noticing the difficulties for content creators to monetize their impact and the lack of enough marketing channels for cross-border goods suppliers, we launched MyyShop, venturing into our second revolution.

Diane at MyyShop's launch event

MyyShop is a pioneering social commerce platform that provides an effortless selling experience on social media, including an e-learning platform that offers social commerce knowledge and skill building, and a comprehensive set of services like logistics and payment, which are necessary for any e-commerce business.

Different yet alike

About ten years ago, I began visiting more of our customers globally, and that was when I realized how many female customers were on our platform. Although their backgrounds and their countries of origin differed, they had one thing in common. That was that these women shared the same goal to start their own business with the help of e-commerce and the power of the internet.

Before the internet, reaching those goals would have been difficult. Flexibility in a woman's work and life is limited, and so are opportunities for achievement. Now, I realized, our e-commerce platform was helping many women become entrepreneurs and reach their true potential. Finally, they were able to become more independent because e-commerce provided them with the flexibility they had previously lacked.

As I became acquainted with these women, I could see that we were as alike as we were different. In this diverse group, some were drawn to e-commerce because it provided them with a way to survive that was previously unavailable to them. Others saw it as I had as a young woman when I left the multinational companies as a successful executive, because I wanted not only outward but also inward success. All of these women saw e-commerce as a way to be creative and to achieve. They are examples of my goal to serve others, not only through the services we provide but also by the opportunities we are able to open for other women.

Diane with creators in LA

THE UNITED STATES: FROM PROFESSOR TO ENTREPRENEUR

At a US focus group, I met Joanne, a university professor who was one of our customers. She shared with me that she had opened her online store as a part-time job. After the birth of her first child, she needed more time at home. In the meantime, she knew how to source baby products online from DHgate. Then, on her blog, she shared her parenting experiences and her purchased products. Gradually, more and more new moms trusted her and asked her to help them source different products online. In time, she decided to quit her job as a university professor and rechannel her career to become a full-time e-commerce entrepreneur.

AUSTRALIA: BALANCING HER WORK AND HER LIFE

In 2015, while attending an international conference in Australia, I secretly acted as a delivery person transporting goods to a woman there named Eva. Then, I introduced myself as the founder of DHgate, where she purchased the goods, and we all enjoyed the surprise. She told me DHgate had helped her realize her dream and that her career had allowed her the flexibility to balance her work and life. Although she had a very young daughter, she wasn't willing to be a full-time mom. Fortunately, she learned about DHgate through Google and came up with the idea of importing goods by way of our marketplace and selling locally via an online shop in her free time. As a mother familiar with children's clothes and toys, she knew what to choose on DHgate. She then listed products she had chosen on Facebook—and because she was skilled in product selection, they sold well.

THE MIDDLE EAST: NOT MONEY ALONE

Our colleagues once went to visit Sue, a buyer in Dubai who had a large transaction volume. She has achieved a certain size for her start-up. So, when we went on a business trip there, we found her because we had her sales records. We got the address and wanted to pay a visit. Sue didn't open the door and left only a small window open.

At first, she refused to meet with us, and we left. Ultimately, we explained that we had come a long way, and she changed her mind. After meeting her, we realized she was quite wealthy, unlike many people we see who work to make ends meet. It's not about the money for her. She just finds the work interesting.

NEW GUINEA: CHANGING CAREERS AND LIVES

In April 2016, we traveled to Papua New Guinea to attend a meeting of the APEC Business Advisory Council, and we conducted a local partnering cross-border e-commerce training program. At the training venue, approximately six hundred to eight hundred people showed up. One man carried a pole and was dripping with sweat when he arrived. Another rowed his boat to shore and came in barefoot. When we told them about cross-border e-commerce, they all bemoaned the fact that global trade could be made in this way. One of the farmers who planted coffee and lamented the interference of the middlemen had no idea that their coffee could be directly put online for buyers to purchase in China, Latin America, and Europe. The local population is about seven million, and at that time, the internet penetration rate was only 2 percent. Imagine how e-commerce changed many careers there.

NIGERIA: NO PREVIOUS EXPERIENCE

A Nigerian woman named Miriam came across MyyShop, enabling her to participate minimally in global trade. Word of mouth is a powerful way to influence people in Nigeria, and Miriam, a college graduate, is trusted by her local friends. She easily gained followers in her community. With no previous experience, she opened a store using MyyShop. Then, based on artificial intelligence (AI) recommendations, she quickly selected the products she wanted and shared product-recommending links with her friends. Once her friends clicked the buy button, MyyShop managed the cross-border payment and logistics services, delivering the goods to her buyers directly. The mother and child products she recommended were so popular that sales reached USD $50,000 only six months after she started the business. As I completed this book early in 2023, she believed sales could reach USD $1 million that year. And all of this with no previous experience.

I celebrate the success of these women, and I am driven by the excitement of achievement and by my goal to change the world. In traditional industries, it was impossible for a woman without resources to achieve success. Through innovation and creativity, these women—and you—can do something different and benefit others.

I am not satisfied with only providing a platform to enable more entrepreneurs. In the future, we can have two weapons. One is hard skills, and the other is soft skills, such as emotional intelligence and listening to your instinctive voice within. I hope to motivate more people, particularly women, to reach their unlimited potential. We can achieve more together.

As technology develops, the opportunities for all of us are evolving and unprecedented. Looking forward, I am excited about what we can achieve in the next three to five years and beyond with new business models and new battlefields.

Connection

Many years ago, it was difficult for women to reach the senior level in a traditional company, and it was almost unreal to be able to do business in more than 225 countries and regions. Imagine, 225 countries and regions! How many traditional industry companies in the world have such a wide range of business? We now have businesses around the world, many of which you may not even have heard of.

I am now still living in the second revolution with DHgate, the social commerce era. I see the essential power of digitalization as *connection.* It connects individuals with someone they might not ever meet in the traditional world. It also makes it much easier to share information, resources, and even business opportunities. The connection power of digital far exceeds the limitation of the physical world. And women everywhere are part of it.

Reflection exercise

- Which story in this chapter resonates with you?

- How does it make you feel about your own potential?

- After reading this chapter, what do you think are essential attributes for entrepreneurs?

- What does the concept of connection mean to you?

- What are your thoughts about serving others? How might serving others connect to your personal goals as an entrepreneur?

Next

Now that you can see the many opportunities for success, perhaps you're ready to go to battle. But wait! Be sure your focus is on action and not reaction.

CHAPTER 3

We Can't Win If We Fight the Wrong Battle

If you are sitting around the table but you say nothing, that's a lost opportunity. Move beyond that and say something about what you have to offer. The reason you're there is because you have something valuable that can be added.

—Ursula Burns, CEO of Xerox Corp

Breaking the glass ceiling. There's much to admire about this phrase at first glance, much that has probably made it a call to action for many of us. Imagine Wonder Woman, perhaps—this larger-than-life woman, fist outstretched, as she aims to shatter that ceiling and let the shards of glass rain down as she soars even higher, blazing a path for other women.

Does that really sound like a woman you know or want to be?

When did you first hear about the concept of the glass ceiling? For me, it was when I worked at Microsoft. Here's the *Merriam-Webster* definition: "an intangible barrier within a hierarchy that prevents women or minorities from obtaining upper-level positions." In other words, qualified women can't advance until they break through something, however intangible, designed to keep them from succeeding.

The term was created in 1978 by writer/consultant Marilyn Loden at the Women's Exposition in New York. From 1991 to 1996, through the Glass Ceiling Commission, the US Department of Labor studied the phenomenon and how it affected women and minorities in the workforce. In 1995, the commission found that white men held most management positions in corporations and that the workforce was divided, with women and minorities accessing fewer leadership opportunities.[1]

Although many speak about the benefits of women participating in the economy and women in C-suite positions, recent data shows that there have been no substantial changes. The reality is that companies are reluctant to add females in high-end positions. According to the 2022 BRICS Women's Business Alliance Development Report, globally, the proportion of women on the board of directors ranges from an average 22.6 percent in Europe to 14.2 percent in the United States, while it is generally low across Asia.

Some people blame education or lack of it for the inequity. In the United States, there are more college-educated women in the workforce than college-educated men, yet women lag behind in pay and opportunity. China's Compulsory Education Law, which

---

1   Melanie Lockert, "Understanding what the glass ceiling is and how it affects women in the workplace," businessinsider.com, March 10, 2022, https://www.businessinsider.com/personal-finance/glass-ceiling.

was implemented in 1986, balanced education inequality; however, inequality still exists.

Others say that women are simply not aggressive enough to break through the glass ceiling, yet in actual practice, calling a woman "aggressive," especially in a performance review, is not a compliment and can harm her chances of promotion: "An article in the *Harvard Business Review*, which looked at 200 performance reviews within one company, revealed bias in this type of feedback. The results tallied the number of references to being 'too aggressive' in the reviews and, not surprisingly, 76% of the instances were attributed to women, while only 24% of men were identified as having such a communication style."[2]

Women frequently have numerous obligations and commitments at home. The major responsibilities of caring for housekeeping and childcare fall on them. If a company schedules impromptu meetings and expects upper management to adhere to hectic schedules, including late-night socializing with clients and co-workers, it might be—consciously or not—signaling that women in leadership don't fit the company culture.

Writing for the *Harvard Business Review*, Debra Meyerson and Joyce K. Fletcher say, "Most organizations have been created by and for men and are based on male experiences. Even though women have entered the workforce in droves in the past generation, and it is generally agreed that they add enormous value, organizational

---

2   Pratima Rao Gluckman, "When women are called 'aggressive' at work," Forbes. com, August 28, 2018, https://www.forbes.com/sites/nextavenue/2018/08/28/ when-women-are-called-aggressive-at-work.

definitions of competence and leadership are still predicated on traits stereotypically associated with men: tough, aggressive, decisive."[3]

As you probably know, the so-called ceiling is simply a carryover from earlier times (as far back as the Bronze Age in China) when men were so greatly valued over women that boys were given more nutritious food than girls. This mindset passed over to agricultural society, then industrial society, and finally, the information era.

My concept of the glass ceiling evolved over time. I found myself beginning to question why women *needed* to try breaking a system that was designed by men. Many are obsessed with fighting the glass ceiling, but if you fight in a system designed by others, you tend to lose. That doesn't mean that some women who have fought haven't made breakthroughs; they have. But what is the cost? Michelle Bachelet, the former president of Chile, once told me that she was supported and elected because of a photo of her wearing an army uniform in front of a tank.

If you have to assume traits that are not yours, stick to habits that are not yours, and dress in a manner that is not yours, what have you truly won? Men may not be from Mars and women from Venus as John Gray's popular book title suggests, but as his book theorizes, we are different species with different characteristics and advantages. I soon came to realize that the external environment might be too complicated for women to change, let alone control, in a short period of time, especially in countries with long-lasting cultural taboos regarding women and work. I also realized that as long as we can realize our own advantage, that is enough. Our advantage lies in our ability to connect, and we need to give full play to that. Women have

---

3   Debra Meyerson and Joyce Fletcher, "A modest manifesto for shattering the glass ceiling," Human Resource Management, Harvard Business Review, January-February 2000, https://hbr.org/2000/01/a-modest-manifesto-for-shattering-the-glass-ceiling.

the power to rise above treating one another as rivals, and we thrive in systems that feature connection and mutual support.

A different way of thinking

In *The Art of War*, Sun Tzu writes, "The supreme art of war is to subdue the enemy without fighting." What if we apply that to the career and personal paths we choose? What if we turn away from the concept of a glass ceiling and turn within? Our inner thoughts. Our inner strengths. Our inner dreams. I believe the biggest obstacle for women is not from the outside but, in most cases, from the inside.

The first thing to conquer is your feelings of limitation. If you can gain energy and pursue what you want inside, you will find the energy and power to grow yourself to what you want to become.

This is what I discovered at the beginning of my career. There was a glass ceiling. I knew my male counterparts could have an easier time getting a position and that females needed to prove themselves capable numerous times. More than that, though, I also knew that complaining would drain my energy and put me even farther from my goal. My approach was, *OK. This time I did not get the promotion, and I'm going to prove myself again while I keep learning all I can.* I'm not saying I had or have only positive feelings, but I've had very few negative feelings because I intentionally adjust my mood from negative to positive.

MEN SUFFER TOO

Problems with structures like the glass ceiling are not limited to women. Once a man decides to fight a system that he did not create, he also loses. Not every man wants to battle his way to success. Some are drawn to nonprofit work, while some to the arts. Others just want to stay home and nurture their children. The system doesn't work for them, either.

So, let's stop blaming the glass ceiling and the boys' club. Let's stop blaming the outer energy and release the inner energy. And please let's ignore the temptation to get into a fight we didn't start in a game we didn't design. Ultimately, we aren't a bunch of angry, driven people attempting to step on one another as we try to break a metaphorical ceiling that only distracts us from the myriad possibilities available to us—as individuals.

We can make progress without fighting, but we cannot "lie flat," doing nothing. I prefer to think of us as seeds, each of us with our own seed plan. We can be grass or tree, but many want to be a tree instead of grass because diversity is not valued in society. The only way for grass to grow taller is to help the grass shoots grow by pulling them upward, but is it a good idea? If you are a blade of grass, you can enjoy being a blade of grass. If you are a flower, you can enjoy being a flower. If you are an ancient tree that has existed for a thousand years, you can enjoy being an ancient tree. We can all nurture one another.

Empowerment through sharing

When I'm speaking with other women, although I don't see breaking the glass ceiling as the right battle to fight, I do want to talk about what we *can* do. In 2015, Cher Wang, a Taiwanese entrepreneur, co-founder and chairperson of HTC Corporation and integrated chipset maker VIA Technologies, handed over to me the chair of the APEC Women's Leadership Forum. Wang is one of the most famous women in computer technology. A quote of hers that resonates me is this one:

"If you have a vision, no matter how difficult things are, everything just becomes a process."

Diane与女性早餐会参会代表合影

Diane at APEC event

As an entrepreneur, I'm always focused on the concrete versus the conversational. Talking is important, but so is listening, and so is doing. I don't want to just talk about policy recommendations without taking action. I'm more inclined to "do before speak" when it comes to women's empowerment. I also consider the questions that many of us in the field wrestle with. How do we empower women and really make positive changes for women in need? How do we leverage our expertise, such as digital tools, to bridge the digital gender divide? How do we put our ideas into action? I often felt it was an evolving journey as we attempted different ways in my participation in various international organizations and women empowerment task forces.

For example, I organized women's luncheon events four times a year in a host economy of APEC. We started it in the form of informal, free chats during lunch and dinner time and gradually transformed it into a regular, formal group discussion on different topics. For each meeting, I needed to deliver the opening or closing remarks. I was under great pressure to stand behind the podium and talk to so many famous and powerful leaders representing twenty-one APEC economies. I was honored to be in such good company.

For each event, I invited political leaders and local female entrepreneurs to attend panel discussions to understand the real challenges and issues in different economies. As I shared, I think women's empowerment is an evolving process—a gradual process of visibility, conversations, dialogues, resources, and recognition. This process is not restricted to one gender. Involving male leaders and entrepreneurs in the process is necessary to fix the problem from the grassroots level if they have the same level of awareness of gender equality and understand the importance of women's empowerment. When there are more male political leaders joining and endorsing the efforts, we gain more resources and power to make changes in different initiatives.

Using this approach, I expanded these women's empowerment initiatives from a small circle to a bigger one. At one luncheon, Katherine Rich, the CEO of the New Zealand Food and Grocery Council (FGC) and New Zealand Representative in ABAC (APEC Business Advisory Council), told me she was inspired because hearing me speak helped her realize how many resources were available to her in her organizations, in her communities, and in her country, and she would also like to do similar things and motivate and inspire women by standing up and speaking out.

In return, she inspired me as well. From Katherine's feedback, I realized that even though I was once under great pressure to address a group of powerful women and men, there was value in speaking up, even if my words helped only one or two people. In addition, I came to know that we need such mutual understanding and support. Without them, we would not go far. There are many Katherines in many economies. They have resources, and if they want to help other women, we can progress greatly. The problem is that many women still choose to remain silent.

My entrepreneurial mindset dictates how I approach problems in business and in women's empowerment issues. In start-ups, we are constantly verifying ideas and proving them in the market. I will come up with an idea to address a problem, introduce a product or service, and see whether it can solve the problem. It's in my DNA, a combination of the innovative and the practical. This is my ultimate formula to address a problem: test an idea in the market.

Ultimately, I know that we can't rely on anything outside. We must rely on our inner strength. What's important here, I think, is that men, their expectation of us, and their male-constructed glass ceiling should not be our focus. Our focus should be ourselves. So many women struggle with self-limiting beliefs that they hesitate to pursue certain goals because they lack confidence in their ability to succeed.

These mindsets may have originated in family, educational, and/ or societal limitations. That brings me to this question. How well do you know yourself? You are certainly more than a person heading toward a goal that may or may not be one of your own choosing. This is where listening to your heart comes in—again. This is also when you need to have a conversation with the only person who can truly discover your strengths and your path; that person is you.

Tell yourself: "I am an experiment."

Think about the freedom this way of thinking can give you. As I mentioned earlier, we are like seeds never meant to create the same blossoms, flowers, or fruits. You do not need to gain recognition from the outside. You need to recognize—and accept—yourself from the inside. If you do not recognize yourself, how can anyone else? If you do not recognize yourself, how can you or anyone truly accept you for who you are? And how will you know what you really want to do? So take a little time. Visit yourself. Think about it.

If you want to be a stay-at-home parent, do that, just be, and enjoy your life. If you want to be a general, then, of course, you can make that your goal and focus on it. This does not contradict the pleasure of being your true self, as long as you remove the "fighting" mentality from your mindset and focus on the inner you.

Choosing *not* to fight can be the best state. Not fighting means that you have your own belief system. It's a two-step process. First, you have to know and find the truth of yourself, and then you must keep exploring who you are. There are many ways to accomplish both of these goals. I believe that to truly know yourself, you need to connect with nature, the universe, and the endless energy available to all of us. We're open to that when we're young, but often we close our hearts when we suffer defeat and pain in the real world as we grow from the freedom of idealistic childhood into adulthood. We need to open ourselves up again, to trust our intuition, and to know that self-knowledge—the awareness of our attributes, abilities, passions, and motivations—is our superpower.

Once you start to renew your self-knowledge to discover or even rediscover the power you were born with, you can be a determined person, with your own principles, without struggling to gain external recognition. You can grow into a sense of satisfaction and even happiness. Knowing who you are can be a game changer. When you see your own beauty and your personal values, when you realize who you really are, you can then release the whole energy of yourself, and you stand firmly. You can just focus on your own path. You will not worry about the outside or care whether your goal is nearby or far away.

I often think of the story about the old fishermen who came from the same village and fished together as children. One wanted to see the outside world at a young age. The other stayed the same. When the traveler retired, he came back to the village. These two men chose their own paths, beginning at the same point and ultimately reaching the same destination. Yet, the distinct choices they made resulted in different experiences. Although the men may look similar, their perceptions—based on their experiences—differ greatly.

I have handled various roles in different workplaces, from junior positions in multinationals to the top post in DHgate. Experience has taught me that many of us may not recognize how important it is to explore our authentic selves. Believe me, this exploration is essential for all of us. I've made my own attempts at DHgate. I am an experiment in myself. I set an example for our employees, nearly half of whom are female, including those at different levels of management.

We have provided skills training, such as presentation and public speaking, for both men and women to grow. But, in fact, skills do not matter that much. The most important thing is that women need to dare to stand up and speak out. Many women are constrained by their own mentality and consider themselves as "not good enough." Yet, once a woman dares to speak, her enthusiasm can easily influence others, even if her skills are still developing. As long as a woman breaks her cognition barrier, her skills come naturally.

Fundamentally, we at DHgate recognize the role of women deep in our hearts without considering their roles or titles. For example, Serene Jiang is a young, energetic female colleague in our company. Although she joined DHgate quite recently at an entry-level position with very little e-commerce experience, we had her present MyyShop at our annual Seller Conference in July 2022, one of our key events. She surprised us with an excellent presentation, which assured her many responsibilities after that.

Diane with women employees at DHgate

I'm also proud that more than 55 percent of the professionals of the industry on DHgate marketplace are women. Most importantly, I encourage women colleagues to break limitations set by themselves; mindset changing is the most important change. It unlocks all the doors so that you're no longer looking up at the ceiling.

When I had my first child, I breastfed her wherever I could—a bathroom, a warehouse, an office. If I have any regrets, it's that I didn't have enough time to enjoy my daughter when she was a baby, and I've tried to change that for parents who work with us. At DHgate, we have dedicated nursery rooms in our office to provide a safe and secure space for breastfeeding mothers. We encourage and organize activities to enable men and women to bring their children to the office. We also send gifts to the children to let them know how loved and missed they are. When I see children walking or running in our workplace, I'm happy.

I continue to encourage women (as I hope I am encouraging you) to break limitations they have set for themselves. Once that happens, we can move to the important step of focusing on our goals.

FOCUS

Kobe Bryant was focused on becoming the greatest shooter, so he practiced one thousand shots each day without worrying about what he had accomplished yesterday or what he might be able to reach tomorrow, only focusing on what he had accomplished that day. One year later, he became the best shooter in the NBA.

All you have is today. Live in the moment, and stay focused on your own path. That's not always easy, but the more you practice, the easier it will be to gain control over your emotions. Your thoughts will no longer be overwhelmed by regrets about the past or anxiety about the future.

Once you reach success, you'll see your next steps, and they won't all be about you. They will be about the future, and they will be about others.

DON'T BUILD FOR BIG; BUILD FOR GOOD

First, be built for good, not for big. Big is a bit of a myth, and it isn't the only good thing. Supporting your family and helping others don't require you to be big. Being good for society and the community is a major success and has little to do with big.

I used to think that inside a company, employees needed to be as ferocious as wolves and tigers to beat others for survival, and externally, companies either won by swallowing others or lost by being eaten up.

As I look back, I realize we were also like ants on a pilgrimage. In other words, we were completely purpose-driven. On a pilgrimage, as long as you stay committed to the path you've chosen, you get there. It is like the first mountain peak. As I climbed that first mountain, I felt for a while that we had achieved some success. But in the past one or two years, I have realized that the definition of success may be of a single dimension. For example, you have climbed this mountain, but then you realize there are higher peaks to conquer. It's as if you are playing an endless game, and you are always dealing with anxiety.

Becoming rich quickly is something the media talks about a lot, and that is apparently the definition of success. But we are growing slowly to go fast. Seeking success is an endless journey. Like those ants on a pilgrimage, enjoy the climb as you anticipate the next peak.

Our philosophy is helping others succeed, and we have enabled MSMEs and now online influencers and creators to grow their businesses. My idea of serving others is related to my purpose-driven attitude.

First, we are focused on empowerment. We want to create the win-win. That's the foundation of our business model.

Second, we are building a healthy and sustainable business with a solid foundation.

Third, we value employees' well-being. Each can grow with the support of others. Many are willing to shed light to enlighten others' lives and works.

As for rewarding, we reward not only those with good key performance indicators (KPIs) but also those who help others during work as we emphasize teamwork and win-win. If what you care about is only success or failure, you will attract people who also only care about success or failure. If you care about supporting others, you will attract people similar to you.

> On the first level, listen to your heart. On the next level, do things you like to do. On the ultimate level, not only find things you like to do, but bring along others as well.

At some point, you don't want to just grow yourself. You want to help other people. If you can be yourself, not trying to be someone you're not, you can enjoy your life and help others to be themselves and serve others as well. That's the ideal state, the true success.

When I was in the early stage of my career, I was modest and humble at the workplace, not because my culture tends to praise modesty. I treated myself as a trainee or an apprentice. I'm willing to take more hands-on jobs to learn more from others, even about entry-level tasks, such as serving water and welcome snacks. The management team of our company had a 55 km trekking tour in the Dunhuang Gobi Desert in early September 2022. I was on one of the leading teams to finish the trekking adventure first. Standing by the finishing line, I wanted to hug every colleague who also overcame the trekking tour challenge. I wanted to serve them water and snacks and to tell them how unique each one of them is and how very proud I am of them.

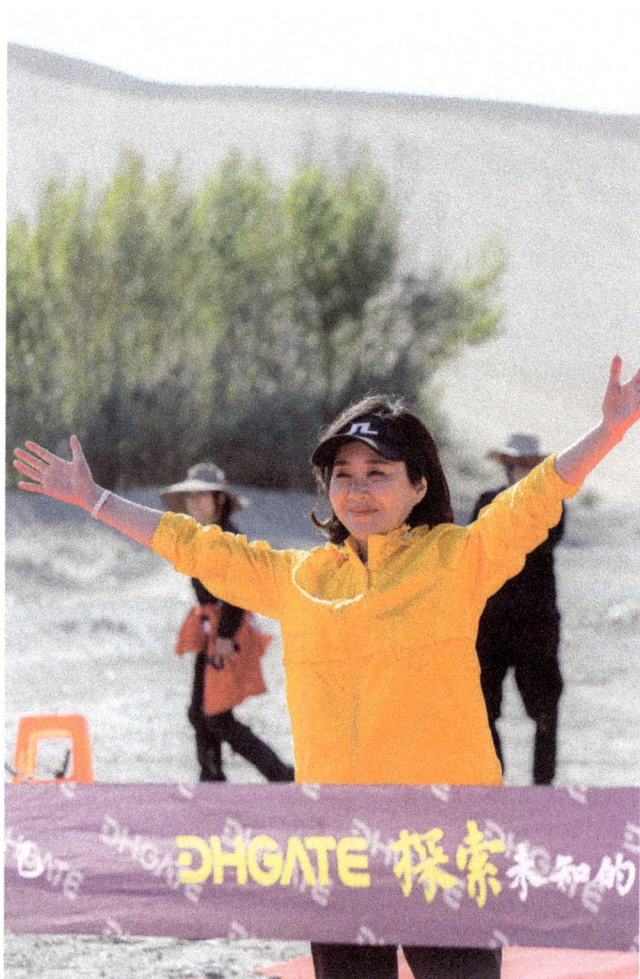

Diane congratulating finishers at Dunhuang

So, two different Dianes—the novice and the founder and CEO of DHgate Group. Thirty years ago, my mindset was modesty and humility because I was still a novice, the "small self." Today, with many rich experiences, I feel my mindset has shifted to be more about my "big self" or "true self," when I hope to serve my colleagues water and snacks with gratitude.

Looking forward to the future, I feel I am discovering my "true self." It's like a calling or a "sense of mission" that motivates me to serve others, encouraging and supporting people and helping them become better.

Reflection exercise

For a moment, think about yourself as an experiment. What parts of this experiment are working for you? What has this experience shown you about yourself so far? Shift your focus from what others are keeping you from doing to what you are and what your heart tells you will make you happiest. What do you see? How does it make you feel? If you could share one thing you've learned on your journey with others, what would it be?

Next

This chapter has been about connecting to your true self and refusing to fight in a battle created by someone else. Next, we're going to look at how to deal with that narrow version of success.

CHAPTER 4

Reframing the Narrow Definition of Success

Strength does not come from physical capacity. It comes from an indomitable will.

—Mahatma Gandhi

One of the exciting parts of being in an evolving career and field is the freedom to change your definitions and ideas about almost anything. For me, and perhaps for you, looking at the definition of success might be an example of that flexibility.

As you know, the usual definition of success is simply about high growth. This so-called success definition is too narrow. We work from nine o'clock in the morning to nine o'clock in the evening, six days a week, which means everyone competing with us is doing the same thing. Yes, that's a lot of unhealthy competition. A financial crisis is another kind of endless competition. We're in a mindset of limitation, not prosperity. There's only so much to go around, we tell ourselves, so we have to keep everyone else from getting theirs so that maybe we can get ours.

Sometimes we forget about why we're here, and it's not to fight against one another. In the last days of his life, Steve Jobs had regrets because he had fought the wrong battles. Or so say unofficial news stories. Whether Jobs actually spoke the quotes attributed to him is something we'll never know. Here's something we do know he said, however, because he said it as part of his 2005 commencement address at Stanford University. It deals with the fact that moving forward requires you to put your trust in something—including yourself: "Again, you can't connect the dots looking forward; you can only connect them looking backward. So you have to trust that the dots will somehow connect in your future. You have to trust in something—your gut, destiny, life, karma, whatever. This approach has never let me down, and it has made all the difference in my life."[4]

What can you do with those twelve hours you were going to spend in the office fighting a battle you didn't want and didn't create? Why aren't we asking this question of ourselves and others? Instead, we're talking about how fast we can grow a company. Big isn't the only good thing. Supporting your family and helping others don't require you to be big. Being good for society and the community is also success.

So, the reason we come into the world may be that we want to have experiences and we want to taste life. Yet, if we are running every day, we have no time and no room to enjoy life or explore its real meaning. At different stages of my career, I had a different understanding—and relation to—what I thought of as success.

---

4   "'You've got to find what you love,' Jobs says," Stanford News, June 12, 2005, https://news.stanford.edu/2005/06/12/youve-got-find-love-jobs-says/.

Four stages to define success

In stage one, I defined success as getting more *responsibility and, along with it, more recognition.*

Around the time I entered the workplace in Tsinghua University, my success definition was something like this: *If I perform well, my boss will give me more responsibilities, I can then learn more things, and I also get more recognition if the results of my work are good.*

In stage two, success was about getting a *promotion to leadership.*

When I worked for Microsoft, I was keen to deliver business performance results. I wanted to be promoted, to be a people manager, to lead a team, and then enlarge my scope of work to get promoted even higher. That worked for me at the time. I managed to become the youngest manager to be promoted in a very important department, and the youngest Chinese mainland employee to be promoted as head of the department. At Cisco, our team was recognized by headquarters as the best in Asia at the time. I felt that eventually I would be promoted as the country manager, the general manager of a multinational company. And I asked myself, *So what?* There were many multinational companies, and I wanted to do something unique.

In stage three, I related success to *thinking big and working hard to realize that dream.*

When I left Cisco to start Joyo, I thought success meant that you can think big, and you can work hard to realize that dream. At that stage of my life and career, I did know that I wanted to do something different. Later, I realized that I wanted to contribute to making the world a better place; I wanted to serve others.

In stage four, and perhaps stage five in the future, success, for me, is defined as *not to build for big but build for good at my own pace.*

When I started my first business, we had no resources; we had to start from scratch. Yet, I was beginning to think big, not only about my business and the milestones I wanted to achieve but also about my ultimate goal to make the world a better place. Then, my state of mind changed, and I realized that climbing mountain after mountain to achieve success was an endless game.

A platform for personal growth

Those were my four steps of success—from the university to Microsoft, to Cisco, to my first business, to now, with DHgate. Today, for me, to win or lose is not enough. I want to bring others with me to spread that energy. I've come to realize that if I stand up, if I speak out about my vision, the amazing thing is I can attract more resources to myself.

Many of these people want to accomplish something similar, and they need somebody to build a platform so that they can realize it. I am willing to dedicate myself, be one of the first joining the camp who has also committed to this mission, to stand up and speak out, and build a platform so that we can gather more power altogether. My dream, which is the foundation of my business, is to not only treat the workplace as that—a *place* to *work*—but also as a platform for personal growth, a place where people can support their family and friends and also find and share their inner energy. We are good at building a platform, integrating various resources from different places, and matching people with different capacities and needs.

Once the platform to serve others is established, it can be a magnet to attract a wide variety of people sharing the same energy, frequency, or vibration. As the platform proves its reliability over time, more people can join and contribute as well.

I think what happened to me is similar to Abraham Maslow's hierarchy of needs, which is really a theory of motivation. The five needs in his pyramid are physiological, such as food and shelter; safety; love or belonging; esteem; and, at the top, self-actualization. Although his research, which focused on notable, educated white men, and his belief that progression on the pyramid had to be linear are criticized today, I believe the pyramid concept is useful, especially when we realize that self-actualization is ongoing and not a single destination.

I stayed in the level of self-esteem for a long time, and I see others doing that as well. They need the applause, the recognition. We all do to some degree, but at some point, we need to move beyond that. As long as you hold esteem for yourself, you have a foundation to move to self-actualization. You don't need verbal praise because you understand who you are. You're like the tree that has survived for thousands of years and has its roots deeply planted in the earth. You are, in the best sense of the word, grounded.

Even if you're a struggling student or anyone trying to meet basic needs (physiological or safety) in your life, you can still practice exploring what your higher needs are, and you should.

I stay focused on my own path in building a platform to serve others and answering my calling in life. As for the success of a company, I think that can be of three dimensions.

The first is commercial value. It is about scale and profitability. It is the basis for a company to *remain a stable, sustainably innovative operation that promotes staff well-being.*

The second is about social value. It is critical for a company to do meaningful things giving back to society and bringing value to its employees so that they can enjoy rewarding personal growth in a supportive environment while making a decent living. This value should also be extended to external partners.

The third is about staff well-being. It is critical in stage four that we hope to help our employees realize their unlimited potential, to achieve personal growth at work and in life on our platform.

Stage four and beyond

In my view, success in stage four and beyond is mostly beyond DHgate, beyond this single company, beyond its business value, its value for employees, as well as its social value, and it is about serving others, mostly externally. Stage four could incline more to the community development we mentioned earlier or be about the ecosystem where our company is located, including merchants on our platforms, MyyShop users, and ex-DHgate employees. Our ambition is to build a family or a platform where different stakeholders who share the same passion can support and learn from one another. My goal is to create an environment of peace, harmony, and happiness, a place for mutual benefit and growth together.

Pacing, not chasing. Mandarin: 从容, or Conrong

When you're firm about what you want to do, as I was with my business, you don't have to be in a rush. You keep your own pace. You want to do it from your heart, and you feel peaceful, confident, and relaxed.

> *Pacing, but not chasing: You do not chase. If you pace yourself, you can move farther in the long run.*

That's where I am with my current project right now. There's a rhythm to it that feels like this: *Never stop, never rush. Keep going. Achieve some progress, maybe bigger, maybe smaller. But as long as we are on the way, that's the right pace.* We are pacing our success, not chasing anyone or anything.

We're told if we're to become successful, we have to step it up, yet we've all seen many burn out by following that advice. I'm not saying you need two weeks of doing nothing; I know that wouldn't work for me. I spend probably 70 percent of my time on business operations, including building the new platform to serve others. I feel good about my current state of life. I have affirmative goals, I am passionate about what I do, I'm not working as hard as I did in the past several years, but the results are getting better and better.

I spend the other 30 percent of my time on learning, personal growth, spiritual matters, and exercise. After a whole day at work, sometimes I feel a headache coming on, but after two to three hours of badminton, I'm fine.

Buddha's statue from Diane's trip to Yunnan

Meditation also helps you practice letting it go. During the Spring Festival, I came across a small temple in Yunnan province, where I saw a Buddha statue. Its hand gesture drew my attention, and I felt like it was telling me to let it go and give love. The pacing helps you enjoy the process. Part of that pace is recharging; part of it is sharing the energy. If all you're thinking about is winning, you're thinking of everyone else as potential losers. If you are on the right path, then distance, speed, size, and winning do not matter. Enjoy the process.

So what is joy? I think it has many layers.

- Short joy: This kind of joy is brief and enjoyable. It might come from enjoying a good meal or a massage. It could be the simple joy of shopping with your friends.

- Longer-lasting joy: This is satisfying but not deep joy. You experience it when you achieve at work or feel a sense of harmony.

- Even longer and deeper joy: This is when you talk to your heart. It's when you find and act on your passion. It's also when you find inner peace and peace at home.

- Ultimate/sustainable joy: This deeply satisfying joy comes when you climb your inner mountain, when you focus on serving others, and when you give back.

These three mantras I try to live by are essential to pacing:

- Optimistic thinking: Expect the best. How you perceive something or someone depends on the angle at which you view them. If you view your situations from a positive perspective, you'll have better results. In my mind, the best is yet to come. Always.

- No bragging, no complaining: Eliminate these two and watch your world get better.

- Persistence: There's no victory, and there is no failure, as long as you keep going. Maybe the path that you're on isn't the right one, but if you keep going, you will discover the right path. The secret is motivation. When you find what brings you joy, you'll be motivated to continue on that path.

One of the first questions I ask people who want to work for me is, "What kinds of things make your eyes shine?" What kinds of things are they particularly interested in or full of passion to do? That's what I need to know because if the motivation and the goals are there, I know what kind of support to provide. At my company, we're currently creating a personal growth plan for employees. What we're really asking is, "In what particular area can we support you to grow?"

I value motivation. I think it's the inner drive that makes people move and work hard. So, I hire people with passion.

We are dealing with cross-culture management seriously. As we have more and more people around the world joining us from different cultures, different time zones, speaking different languages, the challenge lies in how we can bring people from different places together, and engage and motivate them in a way that works for all of them. I am not only proud of the business performance of our team but also that we help one another find personal growth and new capabilities by providing a supportive environment.

One way we encourage and support employees' personal growth is to encourage every one of us in the company to have a "flag," a New Year's resolution. The flag is nothing related to business but about our personal growth area. We ask all staff members, and that includes me, to put a personal flag on workplace messenger, and we run the personal flag program on Lark, a biz chat and collaboration platform. We want to make it transparent and stress-free, so everyone can see it and support one another in this personal growth area. My New Year's flag is that I will start practicing meditation. Hopefully, I can work together with more staff members as we start our personal journey of exploration.

Serving others

This first occurred to me as a calling in my life when watching the 2006 film *Peaceful Warrior*, based on the 1980 novel *Way of the Peaceful Warrior* by Dan Millman. Yes, we can be inspired in just about any situation, and for me, it was a film. It is about Dan, a gifted athlete whose desire for success drives everything he does, with results that don't go well for him. Then, he encounters Socrates, an unusual mentor who teaches him to live in the moment. At the movie's most dramatic moment, when Dan can see Socrates only in his thoughts, the mentor asks him three questions, and Dan answers. "Where are you, Dan?" "Here." "What time is it?" "Now." "What are you?" "This moment." With that, Dan achieves nearly impossible success.

As I watched it, I realized that "now" is all we have, and I wanted to use the moment of my life to serve others. Empowering others makes me feel meaningful. It helps me live a purposeful life. I don't do it to seek a result or recognition from anyone. It is like an engine driving me to take action.

Although it is not success in the usual definition, to benefit others is to benefit yourself. The more you share, the more you receive emotionally, and I believe spiritually; it is a truly positive cycle. This is true for companies as well. Those with a core belief in serving others can develop better, especially in these times, and more importantly, they can be sustainable.

This doesn't mean you can solve everyone's problems, especially when you haven't been invited to. As an entrepreneur, solving problems is part of my everyday life; it's in my blood. In the past, I intuitively provided friends and family members who were complaining to me about something with a "solution" I felt would solve the source of their complaints. They soon stopped turning to me, and I figured out why when I used the same approach with my daughter. Then it occurred to me that she had not complained to me because she did not want my solution to her problem or anything else. She simply wanted me to be with her and to listen. I learned a great deal from that encounter. Now, when someone complains to me, I silence Diane the Entrepreneur Fixer and think about how I can support this person with more empathy, even when I may know exactly where their bottleneck is. To be a listener is as much about love as it is about wisdom. It's a state of mind where you can understand, without judgment, the emotions of another.

So, what is success, after all?

Success usually comes to those who are too busy to be looking for it.
—Henry David Thoreau

We may encounter many defeats, but we must not be defeated.
—Maya Angelou

The ones who are crazy enough to think they can change the world are the ones that do.
—Anonymous

Fall seven times and stand up eight.
—Japanese proverb

Nobody says, "Congratulations, you have achieved self-actualization." There's no degree for that, no certification, and you can't even buy it. Self-actualization is inside, and it's only the beginning.

I could fill a book with definitions of success; people have. Ultimately, the best definition of success is the one you find in your own heart. At the early stages of your career, you must keep asking yourself who you are and what you really want. It's a process of talking to your heart and getting to know yourself better as you find the truth of yourself.

Frankly speaking, anxiety and pressure were once not uncommon for me when I was developing DHgate. Some companies went public and got listed only five to six years after they were established, while other latecomers in the cross-border e-commerce sector grew bigger and faster than us. DHgate did not go public, and many outsiders were wondering what had happened to us.

DHgate is still a private company, but my mind has changed because we have our own pace, and I agree with an ancient Chinese saying, "More haste, less speed."

My secrets for success

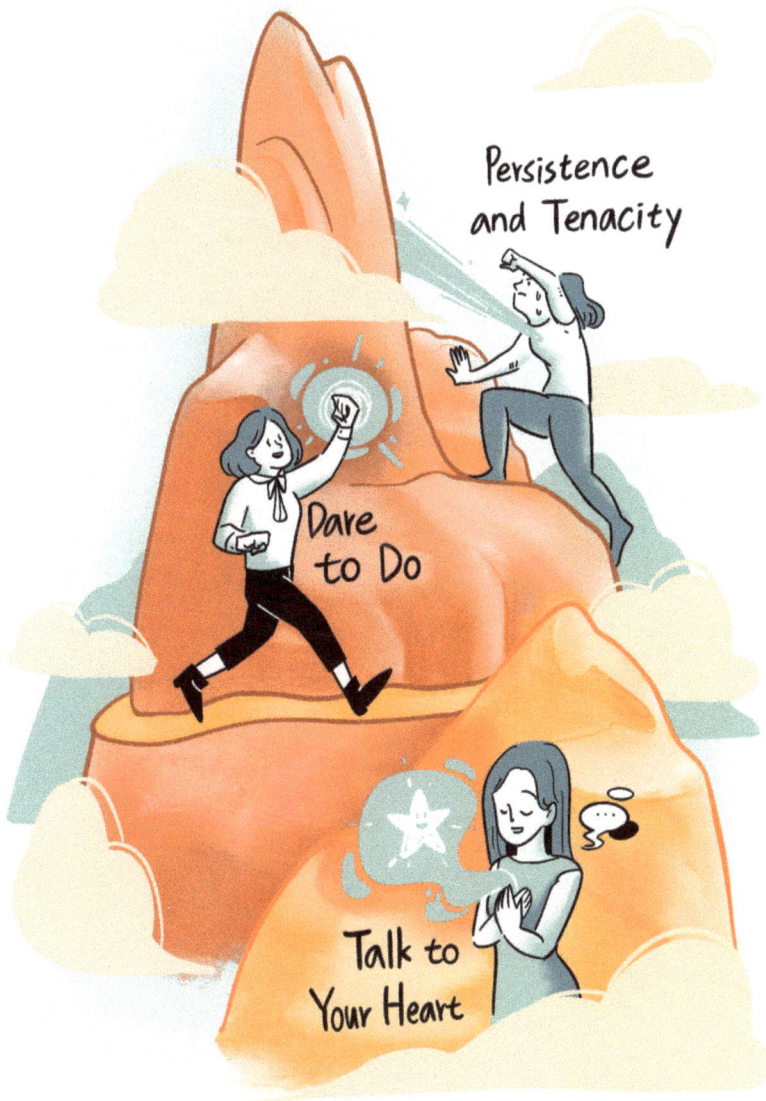

Persistence and Tenacity

Dare to Do

Talk to Your Heart

Talk to your heart

I talk to my heart to find what I am fond of and what excites my imagination; I have done it many times in my life.

Dare to do

Then I take action based on what I learned from my heart.

Persistence and tenacity

I have tenacity in achieving my goals because I am very determined to pursue what my heart tells me. Even when I am on the verge of giving up, when I feel so stuck in the moments when there seems to be no way out and I'm trapped in a corner, my strong willpower, my belief, and my persistence lead me to see something positive, to find the 0.1 percent "silver lining" out of the 99.9 percent overwhelmingly negative.

Once you find that greater understanding, don't struggle to make up for your disadvantages. Instead, focus on developing your advantages to a master level. I'm not just speaking of business either. I'm talking about your true calling in this one life you've been given. If you know yourself better, you will know what you really want—not just what you've been conditioned to want. That knowledge will be your first step to your own definition of success.

Reflection exercise

• What did success mean to you as you began your career?

• What does it mean to you now?

• What role models do you have who exemplify success? Why and how?

• Look at the pace of your life right now. Are you pacing or chasing? How content are you with that? How might you change it?

• Where do you see yourself and your life on Maslow's pyramid?

Next

At the beginning of this book, I mentioned how I can talk to my heart, to listen to my inner wisdom when I need guidance. Now, I'm going to show you how to do that.

CHAPTER 5

Dare to Fail; Dare to Do

Don't be afraid of going slowly. Be afraid of standing still.

—Chinese proverb

Failing doesn't automatically make you a success, but it may be part of the process. In my life as an entrepreneur, I experienced failure before I experienced success. As I mentioned before, my career at Microsoft taught me that patience and high performance could lead me to success but not as fast as I felt I deserved it. That was my first mountain—success in the traditional sense.

Imagine how it can feel to be unafraid of failure. That's the attitude you need to develop because true success rests on the other side of failure. Many have written about how long you must work to develop any talent or skill. Musicians aren't born creating flawless melodies, and artists aren't born creating masterpieces. They achieve that state through practice and failure. If we stop before we fail, we never reach our true potential. So, my advice to you is don't be afraid of failure. Know that it's only a temporary state.

I wish someone had told that to me when I founded DHgate. Although I believed with my heart in what we were doing, success was far from guaranteed. Still, I believed.

Following my inner voice

During the development of DHgate, when the business began to venture into financial services and logistics, the initial challenges we faced were immense. There were uncertainties like risk control and the trade-off between short-term gains and partnerships. I had to make important decisions that would change the course of our business.

Prior to 2008, DHgate collaborated with PayPal, the world's largest online payment platform. As our business grew, we were one of the largest partners of PayPal in the Asia-Pacific at that time. Because I could predict the future development, I proposed to our board the idea of creating our own payment platform at the strategic level. In the past, when I made suggestions, they were generally well received by the board. But this time, I faced the most intense opposition that I can remember. They were completely opposed to my idea.

I can understand the skepticism everyone had. Surely, they were contemplating unspoken concerns such as these: "Who do you think you are? How can this small company compete with a globally successful online payment platform?" While I understood their perspective, considering the circumstances and strategic considerations at that time, I didn't hesitate and was determined to do it. I simply felt, in my heart, that it was the right move.

The outcome proved that it was a right strategic decision. With the rapid development of DHgate, PayPal terminated its cooperation with DHgate. Losing the partnership with PayPal meant losing a powerful tool for expanding into overseas markets, which would impact the growth of cross-border e-commerce trade volume. However, because of our strategic decision, we managed to control performance fluctuations within a manageable range, even maintaining marginal growth, despite a pervasive decline in the cross-border business industry.

Many analysts consider that outcome a miracle. Not me.

I believe that some decisions don't need to rely heavily on data analysis or research. They can come from our own hearts and judgment, allowing us to be more sensitive, intuitive, and determined.

Over the years, we have been constantly trying various new ventures. As you know, the success or failure of entrepreneurial projects is quite common. That's no reason to give up. As entrepreneurs, all we can do is follow our inner voice, put forth our ideas with the best of our abilities, and persist. Whether or not we ultimately succeed is determined by the market and time.

In 2017, we proposed the concept of Social Shop, which was the predecessor of MyyShop. We have been continuously optimizing and iterating, and now MyyShop is still evolving in a rapidly changing market, on the road to success.

THE IMPORTANCE—AND MAGIC—OF PERSISTENCE

When you love and trust yourself, when you listen to your heart, you will experience the confidence that leads to persistence. Although it's an overused word, persistence to me is simply day-to-day repetition. It's not magic at first, but I believe it can create magic.

Here's an example. I wanted to learn English, and I knew I didn't have a lot of free time to do that. Yet, learning English mattered to me, not just for my business but also for my understanding of other people and other cultures. So, here's what I did.

I studied English for twenty minutes a day on an app. I didn't learn it in six months or even a year. I studied on that app for three years, no matter where I was and no matter how busy I was. During those three years, I missed only once or twice. Keep doing something even for twenty minutes each day, and you can see the changes. The main thing is to start. In quoting the ancient Greeks, Aristotle said, "Well begun is half done." Once you begin the process, whether it's studying a language or mastering a physical skill, you have taken a powerful step forward.

As long as the road is long enough

At a young age, I understood the power of persistence. Early in school, I was committed to winning the long-distance relay for my class. The competitors were in a higher grade than we were, but I was determined. Toward the end, I fell, but I kept getting up, telling myself, *As long as the road is long enough, I will be first.* The last runner was a boy, very strong. He was the one I needed to beat. I don't remember how many times I fell at the end, only that I crawled to my destination. And won.

Malcolm Gladwell's book *Outliers: The Story of Success* introduces his 10,000-hour rule, which is that true expertise is achieved by practicing for 10,000 hours. The real key here, of course, is persistence. My studying English twenty minutes a day was the most I could do at that time. Whatever you want may fit in a tiny time frame as well, or you may have more hours a day to devote. Results won't come overnight, but with persistence—and consistency—they will become reality. That doesn't mean your path will be a straight one, and it doesn't mean every success will be a true success and every failure will be a true failure.

Two buckets, one well

Fortune and misfortune are two buckets in the same well. We tend to see only the negative side of a bad situation. Only later do we realize the positive effects that may far outshine the initial negatives.

Sometimes, what seems a setback can bring about significant opportunities. We must remain open to the possibilities that arise from challenges and even failure.

When I look back at my failure with my college entrance examination, I can see it clearly now. First of all, and probably most important, I lacked the confidence to face the exam. Further, the pressure I felt was immense. This single examination would determine the university I could enter. In my young mind, it would determine my future. I was overwhelmed and nervous, and despite my boundless expectations for myself, the pressure I felt hindered my ability to perform at my best.

Once we experience a negative result, it's easy to default to that result again and again, which is what happened to me from middle school to high school examinations to university. I was one of the best students in the Chinese language subject, but I scored only 80. I disappointed my teacher. I used to be her top-performing student, a source of great pride for her. And for me. Ironically, my husband (future husband then, whom I often teased about his Chinese language skills) scored around 110 out of the maximum 120. He wasn't proficient in the subject, yet I scored 30 points lower than he did. That's how poorly I performed.

I've previously mentioned my journey at Microsoft and how I came to realize that some failures could lead to significant opportunities, while certain successes might be preceded by challenges. It all depends on the perception one chooses to adopt. I shared this insight with some of my colleagues who initially joined Microsoft alongside me and, at first, seemed to outperform me. They encountered the same walls I did—walls that were not based on performance—and one by one, they decided to leave and pursue alternative career paths. They didn't fail. They learned, and they grew.

I'm not saying it's easy to choose a different path. If you are connected to yourself, listening for answers and not just taking the easiest approach to challenges, I believe that you will begin to understand your true path. I also think you already know that path, but perhaps your way to it has been blocked by thinking and demands by yourself and others that no longer serve you.

Though initial prospects might not appear auspicious, unforeseen positive surprises may unfold. It's a matter of adopting a particular perspective when assessing any situation. I came to realize that, when you claim success or failure, you've already defined your perspective on what it means to succeed or lose. Your viewpoint shapes your interpretation.

A 360-DEGREE VIEW

During my time at Microsoft, my perspective began to shift. I started to see people—their personalities and their desires—like seeds that have their own plan for growth.

This allowed me to view and value success and failure differently as well. Most important, I realized that some so-called failures could lead to significant opportunities, while certain "successes" might be accompanied by challenges. Ultimately, I realized that true perspective encompasses a 360-degree view of a situation. The power to decide lives within us.

When I shared this insight with some of my colleagues who joined Microsoft alongside me, I was surprised by their responses. Initially, they seemed to outperform me, and their backgrounds were, in my opinion, superior to mine. Yet, when we spoke later, each expressed that they had struggled to accept instances of perceived unfair treatment. Consequently, one by one, they decided to leave Microsoft and pursue alternative career paths. These colleagues viewed their supposed "failure" of unfair treatment differently than I viewed my setbacks in advancing as fast as I wanted to. That experience taught me to look at both sides of the proverbial coin. It taught me to remember that fortune and misfortune are two buckets in the same well.

Do your homework

Sometimes, the process of finding your true path involves homework. One of our veteran staff members who has been developing herself from an assistant role to a department head shared with me that she was frustrated in the workplace. We discussed the importance of doing our homework.

I'm not talking about the homework we did in school. I'm suggesting that during the workday, we have time for only that and little more. Yet, once we are away from work, we have time to reflect. In reality, it's an opportunity for personal growth. Finally, you can experience the emotions like frustration and just plain anger. The homework is about you, though, and not about others. If all you do is ask, "Why?" you'll still be stuck in those negative feelings. Instead, ask,

"What?" What does it mean? What can you learn from the emotions you're experiencing? If all you ask is *why* someone did something to you, you won't learn anything. If you ask *what* you can take from this experience, you'll learn and grow.

True, the homework starts with a negative, but I suggest you look at and reflect on it. I look at anger and frustrations differently now. Instead of immediately engaging in arguments as I once did, I prioritize self-reflection. I explore the underlying causes of my emotions and try to gain insights from the emotions I experience. Today, as I write this book, I can see that I have gone through two stages.

The first stage is letting go of my anger. I consciously shift my focus to the positive aspects of the person involved in whatever conflict I'm experiencing. I remind myself that nobody is perfect, and I also find the positive characteristics in this person. That's the first stage, and the second doesn't follow immediately. I give it a couple of days, if possible.

Then, I enter the second stage, and I'm relieved that the anger has disappeared. Still, there's something unpleasant in my heart that I try to avoid. My inner courage is pushing me to sit down with the person, and I know I must. At this point, I'm interested in exploring the causes, and I can engage in direct conversation with the person. I'm just looking for clarity, discussing the facts. No more labeling, no more blaming. My willingness to enter the second stage is a sign of courage. I'm ready to face conflict with goodwill and intention. The intention is to get away from the why (*Why are you doing that to me?*). Doing the homework has helped me—as it will help you—refrain from emotional reactions, manage our moods, and respond with intention instead of anger.

Build inner strength through practice, and embrace the possibility of making mistakes. Strong leaders show vulnerability. Voicing vulnerabilities is not self-blaming or self-pity. It's a declaration of courage and humanity. If you only want to show you are strong, you take the way of the wolf, and you do your best to weaken and destroy others. On the contrary, if you are not hiding your vulnerability, showing who you really are, you make others strong, because it shows strong self-awareness, and you are honest with the people around you. I'm frequently reminded of the sand analogy. As long as your hand is open, you can hold more sand. If you clench your fingers around it, trying to hold those grains, you will lose most of them. Open is better even when you're not certain of the outcome.

In our everyday lives, people often tend to react in two common ways when faced with conflicts. The first reaction is to *fight*, which causes harm and doesn't address the root of the conflict. The second reaction is to *avoid*. When you are involved in a back-and-forth exchange of arguments and counterarguments, the natural response is to take flight. Both reactions are unhealthy and unproductive.

In these situations, we often find ourselves deeply entrenched in the "why" model, constantly questioning and probing: "Why did you do that?" "Why did you say that?" This endless questioning leads to no resolution.

Instead, you need to stick to the facts. Otherwise, you'll be forever lost in the "why?" To prevent ourselves from getting stuck in the "why" model, we should focus on the facts and approach the situation with good intentions. Instead of avoiding or escaping, we should have open and honest conversations. I can share my feelings, and you can provide me with the factual perspective. Through this connection, we can address misunderstandings and allow the other person to consider alternative approaches in the future. This approach leads to more positive outcomes and fosters deeper understanding and closeness between individuals.

Believe me, this process is a gift, regardless of the type of relationship for which you use it. It allows us to know one another on a deeper level and brings us closer together.

What about you?

Talk to your heart for guidance. Then, take action, whether that is turning left or right, since either way makes sense. If you fail, celebrate failure, learn from it, and move on.

Just put down the weight you carry, and don't push yourself too hard. Avoid self-labeling; define your own success without being confined by the judgments of others. The key is to cultivate a positive self-perception. Be a tree if you wish or a flourishing flower—embrace it and find contentment in your choices. Sometimes we fear that we might fail again or we may not succeed, especially when we have just experienced one or more failures. Past failure is only that. It has nothing to do with who you are or where you are going.

> ### Reflection exercise
> Had I not left my job at the university, I would not have experienced the highs, the lows, the uncertainty, the fulfillment, and great joy my work has brought me. What change could you make that would bring fulfillment and joy to your life?

What's next?

Something that should matter to all of us—self-love.

CHAPTER 6

From Intuition to Self-Love

Nobody can give you wiser advice than yourself.

—Cicero

On a recent trip to our Shenzhen office in East China's Guangdong province, I was surprised to find that some of my colleagues were dealing with anxieties created years before. In several cases, they failed to perform well in those early jobs, and those experiences were still holding them back. Now, in a totally different company, they shared with me that they hesitated to speak up or to innovate. Experiencing failure drained their confidence, limited their potential, and prevented them from personal growth even years later.

I'm grateful those colleagues trusted me enough to share their anxieties with me, and I believe I helped them remove some of the hopelessness they felt. The things that own you are those of which you can't speak. Once you explore them and share in a safe environment, you free yourself. Putting feelings into words is one of the most powerful actions you can take. You hold the helm to lighten your heart and move forward with courage and confidence.

Early conversations leave their imprint

Many times someone asks us something, and we are months, maybe years, away from the answer. Still the question remains. Some conversations and questions may not have immediate answers, but rushing to conclusions is unnecessary and often unwise. The answers will appear to you at the right time.

Looking back, it was years ago when one of my colleagues asked me the question, "Do you feel you're successful?"

The question caught me off guard because I hadn't considered it before, and I wasn't sure how I should respond.

The question caused me to think, however. And the answer came to me: "I'm not successful enough."

Over time, I sensed that something in my career was unaccomplished in my mind, although I couldn't quite pinpoint it. This realization marked the second phase of my awareness: I had achieved a certain level of success, but I still had higher goals to pursue.

Notice that word, but even though I acknowledged some success and evolved my thinking, it still wasn't enough.

The realization is crucial. Consider a half-full glass of water. You can direct your thoughts to the half-full aspect, appreciating what you have and anticipating a full cup soon. Alternatively, you could perceive the glass as still half empty, focusing on what you haven't achieved yet—a full cup. Despite both approaches yielding the same outcome of a full glass, they represent two distinct mindsets, ultimately yielding different outcomes.

Many people are unaware of the influence of their unconscious mind, which can sometimes hinder personal growth. Reflecting on our own success and asking ourselves if we consider ourselves successful are important. It can trigger a shift in thinking and lead to significant outcomes, including how we define success at different times in our lives.

Beyond logic

Listening to your heart goes beyond logical thinking. It also goes beyond intuition, which is instinctive and often visceral.[5] We often listen too much to our brain and not enough to our heart. Both are necessary, and each can serve us well. Both are hindered when we add stress, fear, and worry to the equation. This brings us back to my colleagues in Shenzhen and perhaps to you. Fear hampers both your creativity and your logic. It leaves your analytical abilities fuzzy and your intuitive abilities blocked. And, frequently, it shuts out your heart. When you fear, you don't trust, and when you don't trust, you are unable to hear the wisdom of your heart.

This wisdom goes beyond mere experience because experience alone, as in the case of my colleagues, is not always a true teacher. Experience and research may tell you one thing, but you might wake up one day and say, "I must do this. It is the one thing that will make me happy." That's when you listen. Your heart will never lie to you; your body can feel the truth. First, you need to release the fear. You need to trust and to know that the answers are within. And there's a reason for that.

---

5   Dana Santas, "Your intuition is real. Here's how to strengthen it," CNN.com, October 21, 2022.

Fearlessness: The dragon

Many of us, myself included, at different times in our lives, may think we're not good enough. We lack self-confidence and possibly self-love. Those are important qualities to develop because only when we are able to forgive ourselves are we able to forgive others. Just as important, once we accept ourselves, we can feel that connection to one another that we all have. That connection is the source of great strength. Fundamentally, we are all connected; we are not isolated.

Imagine a dragon. What do you picture when you hear this word? A fire-breather? A colorful, celebratory character, perhaps on a kite? Both images are correct. The dragon, which holds great significance in traditional Chinese culture, symbolizes power, good luck, and prosperity. It is also associated with the emperor and signifies his rule and majesty.

Dragon under Chinese discourses

Ancient Chinese emperors were often referred to as the "Son of the Dragon." This bringer of abundance is often depicted with a pearl, which symbolizes wealth. The dragon is also spiritually significant. It is believed to possess supernatural powers. It is even believed to control the weather. It is seen as a guardian of the cosmic order and associated with celestial beings.

The dragon's strength and courage make it a symbol of protection against evil spirits and negative influences. It embodies the harmonious balance of Yin and Yang, representing the interconnectedness of opposites. A dragon can swim; it can run. In our culture, a dragon can do anything.

So, a dragon is a pretty wonderful thing to be. But do you see anything missing here? Yes. In the ancient times, only the emperor could claim the dragon. Ordinary people could not display any image of it, and if they did, they could be punished by death. Not even the queen could wear the image of the dragon; her image was the phoenix. She was royalty, but she could not be the dragon.

That is what was once believed, but it is not the truth. Inspired by this ancient wisdom, I have my own perspective on the concept. Within us, we all have different energy, and we all have the dragon. That's right. Everyone is a dragon. I am. You are. It is there within us, and the way to access it is through your heart.

You must realize your potential and talents, explore your inner spaces, and expand your definition of yourself. Defining your role and self-confidence are essential breakthroughs in the journey of self-discovery. This means not seeking validation from others or conforming to their standards. Avoiding these "shortcuts" lets you focus on your own standards and ignore labels and judgments that others apply to you. The goal is to release your potential and energy, and you can't do that if you're focused on what other people think you should do and be.

As we evolve and recognize the abundance in life, we come to realize that success is not only personal, but it also involves collective collaboration.

What a dragon does for company culture

In some company cultures, there is no room for anything but competition and exclusion. As I'll discuss in the next chapter, those companies have a "wolf" culture. After time and experience, I realized that those concepts are counterproductive to what I choose to achieve.

That was when another question I was asked resonated with me. The question was, "How do you define a company that has a sense of happiness?"

I responded by saying, "It is an environment where everyone embodies the spirit of the dragon." Yes, the spirit of the dragon serves companies as well as individuals. That's because the concept of everyone as a dragon carries with it the idea that everyone has the potential for greatness.

A company with a sense of fulfillment and even joy is one where everyone is empowered and can achieve their full potential. Embracing this concept means that our surroundings and the people with whom we interact influence our perception of our capabilities. There is no corporate "type." When everyone embodies the spirit of the dragon, they need to believe in themselves, which will lead to more varied and more beneficial outcomes.

As mentioned earlier in this book, each person is unique, like various plants with their own growth plans. They can bloom and thrive in their own way. If I am a flower, I am the most vibrant flower. If I'm a tree, I'm not trying to be the most vibrant flower. Everybody in the company doesn't have to be a vibrant flower, nor should they want to be. The challenge is to decide what you want to be. Whether you are a CEO, a salesperson, a secretary, or a cleaner, it is not about what you do but who you are. It's about embracing your own path and living the life you choose to the fullest.

The dragon is a state of being, and I see being in its simplest form as a mindset. In this state of fulfillment, every person embraces their unique qualities and lives their best life. It is not about attacking the competition or one another. It is going within and exploring the self. This doesn't mean you isolate yourself; you simply investigate and discover where you are happiest. With such a mindset, you can even change your attitude regarding your daily commute to work. Suppose it's raining. With one mindset, you'll find the rain annoying, blame it for slowing you down, getting you wet, or creating heavy traffic on the road. Yet, we've all felt the beauty of the rain: the soothing sound, the fragrance. What if you transferred that wonder and appreciation to your drive? Perhaps the sound of rain will bring a feeling of peace to your soul. That kind of mindset will serve you throughout and after your workday.

This isn't something you'll achieve instantly, and it's not something you'll learn by mouthing slogans, regardless of how trendy they are. Self-realization requires genuine action and effort. However, you'll start to notice small changes, and the process will begin to transform you by degrees. Gradually, you'll realize your true self, and the more you explore within yourself and in meaningful conversations with others, the closer you'll be to self-discovery. This will lead to recognizing your capacity for care and compassion, which again will expand your understanding of yourself. This transitioning from self-centeredness to a focus on serving others can be a natural progression in personal growth.

EVERYTHING IS CONNECTED

I believe that in the universe, everything is connected. We are connected to nature and one another. When you truly listen to your heart, you shut out all the noise, both without and within. I think that, fundamentally, human beings have more in common and more similarities than we have differences. Whether a first-year college student or a CEO, we all want love. We all want safety. We all want to be heard and to be valued. No matter how different the outside conditions, the inside conditions remain the same. We all have the freedom to look into our hearts and explore. Even someone in prison can do that. Regardless of your situation or your circumstances, no one can stop you from exploring your heart.

The fundamental element is love

Earlier, I mentioned Maslow's hierarchy of food/shelter all the way to self-actualization. Truly, though, love is less structured, and when you have that, the rest becomes clearer. We begin with self-love. If you don't love yourself, you aren't capable of loving others.

So the first thing is to love yourself so that you have the energy, the compassion, and the capacity. If you love yourself, you understand yourself, and this makes it easier for you to understand others. For instance, I was surrounded by love from family, and this allowed me to take risks. At first, I wasn't sure why I had that confidence, but then, I realized that I could provide this same supportive love to my family members and also to my team. Love gives you security and trust. It gives you courage. It allows you to reach out and share that love with others. Self-love allows you to be more forgiving—of yourself and of others. It allows you to forgive yourself in the face of failure and not allow that failure to morph into shame you carry forward. You know, no matter what may come, that you will be supported. And that is what is so liberating.

Self-love forms the foundation of a harmonious society, fostering personal well-being and cultivating positive connections with the world. A quote attributed to Buddha states, "You yourself, as much as anybody in the entire universe, deserve your love and affection."

I believe that understanding self is crucial and that once you connect with your true self, your life will change. Once you have the insight, you will find the path.

Talking to your heart, and why you don't

Talking to my heart benefits me fundamentally, and I believe it benefits you as well. I'm certain that you too have experienced moments when you just knew the right path to take. Or perhaps you didn't know the right path, but you knew where you wanted to end up; you had a goal and a destination. Maybe you called it instinct. Or perhaps you called it a hunch, a gut reaction, or your higher intelligence. Whatever it is, you feel as if *you just know.*

I believe there's a spiritual as well as a psychological element at work when I talk to my heart. As we've already discussed, it requires trust, it requires introspection, and it is well worth the energy you put into it.

So why don't we talk to our hearts more often? Perhaps we're too busy, or at least, we tell ourselves we are. Perhaps we use our brains so much to calculate that we rely on logical thinking and think that is our best approach. Or we're not focused. When we desire too much in too many directions, the natural voice from the heart can fade away.

It may have been easy to talk to your heart naturally when you were young, but as you age, it might be more difficult to listen because you've been rejecting listening to the voices outside you, and your heart has been wrapped up. As a result, your ability to obtain energy from nature might also have been weakened. The journey is internal, and you can find your way back to that initial trust.

Maybe you're just exhausted. You balance work, family, personal challenges, and responsibilities, and at the end of the day, you've already spent your energy elsewhere; you have no room to go within and simply listen. It's worth doing because the voice in your heart is almost definitely the truth.

Hearing the truth; finding your values and passions

It is your strength. It is your passion. If you can follow that, you will have a better chance to be successful in every way because you will focus on the things you love. By looking within, you can face the doubts that impact your decisions.

I'm not important. I don't deserve to move up. That's the typical limitation for women and many men in the workplace. Listening to your heart will help you hear the true message, and it will help you identify your values and your passions.

When people ask how I overcame challenges in my business, I tell them it was not too difficult because I made choices based on what was right for me. I don't do things based on values I don't hold. When you find your values and passion, you have much greater strength and are more powerful than you can imagine.

There is no right way

From the beginning, I knew I didn't want this to be a book that was so rigid and so narrow that it left out others who could benefit from my message. The following suggestions are just that. When you meditate, do yoga, or pray, you have different guidelines, and you incorporate them into what feels right for you. That's what I'd like this to be.

SIMPLICITY

The increase in complexity associated with modern life has left many of us feeling in over our heads. We overthink and are overwhelmed, stuck in one or both of the two poles of depression and anxiety.

Instead, we need to step back and examine the reasons that led us to where we are and find a new way of operating.

I think the true heart desires are always there. That's where your feelings of hope and your true voice reside. You need to keep it simple. Clear your mind to leave some space for the voice in your heart to speak up. If the voice is speaking up, then there's usually a reason, and you should listen.

SOLITUDE

I started to talk to my heart before I knew about solitude, so I did not have an actual plan. But when I recall my journey over the years, I find I enjoyed a few moments of peace and the solitude of my mind. Try to reach the state of just being yourself. Then, with a quiet mind, you may be able to better hear.

NATURE

As I've already mentioned, for me, a connection with nature helps me talk to my heart. This is a capability carried on from my childhood. Nature does not wear makeup the way humans do, and nature is always like what it is unless it is polluted by humans. Our heart knows what we want, but sometimes it can also be "polluted" by desires for fortune, fame, respect, hatred, jealousy, and fear.

JOURNALING

I once kept a diary, writing down what my heart felt during a day alone. That is one way I explored and communicated with myself in the early times. If journaling doesn't work for you, there are so many other ways to communicate with yourself. Perhaps it's a long walk or a reflective time resting by the lake. The key is when you find a way to talk to your heart, you may uncover a desire you've long buried or perhaps discover something surprisingly new. In stirring these feelings, you may also be motivated to act on them.

MEDITATION

Meditation is one way many of us of different beliefs gain inner peace. It can also be a channel to talk to your heart since it allows you to have a period of "void" time. By way of inhalation and exhalation, you pay attention to your breath and your body. Over time and by practice, you become more sensitive to changes in your body, including your heart.

As I mentioned earlier, people today do not dare to take a moment to clear their minds and think of nothing. Such a "void" moment could be easily considered by many as a waste of time.

While meditation seeks energy from inner strength, talking with others takes a different approach. I think people who talk with others, including mentors, seek some guidance and are, in some cases, even more confused because different people give varying pieces of advice.

Any number of mentors could have given me any multitudes of advice when I began my journey. In fact, many well-meaning people did. However, the advice often says more about the one giving it than the one taking it. Talking with others is a search for energy from the outside. Yes, it has value, but the first step should be from within.

Your way is the best way—for you

As you can see by now, every one of us has a way to connect with our higher self. I believe everyone can find their own way if you believe in the magic and power of talking to your own heart.

Once a person is told how to do something, they will lose the capability to find out how to do that. I learned that lesson as a parent, and I continually see parents comply with society's expectations of high achievement at a young age. Yet, if you tell your children to score high so that they will be accepted by a top-ranked university, how are the children going to find out what is meaningful to them and what they want to do with their lives? They are capable of finding answers and solutions. They will find a way to talk to their hearts by themselves. Your job is to inspire when necessary and to trust them all the time. You'll notice I didn't use the word *push* here. That is not part of inspiration, and it is not part of trust.

Many parents are pushing their kids too hard, hoping they can at least be as excellent as they are. Others are driving their children to fulfill their unfulfilled dreams, such as attending a respected university.

- Don't force yourself or others, especially your children, to do anything. Instead, encourage them to follow their hearts and be themselves. *I always encourage my family, my friends, and colleagues to be true to themselves.* This is not pushing. *It's directing them back within* and letting them know that they can realize their true desires from their hearts. An old Chinese saying goes like this: "Do not do to others what you do not want others to do to you." This is similar to what Socrates advises: "Do not do to others that which angers you when they do it to you." They can make changes and grow when the timing is right. Every flower blooms in its own time. Otherwise, it would not bloom at all.

At work, it's my duty as a CEO to see the potential of subordinates and inspire them to get out of their comfort zone to take on new responsibilities. Through continuous practices, I have learned how important it is to deal with their internal burdens, to let them know they can make mistakes. They need to know that mistakes will lead to lessons learned. They need to know that you will always trust them. Telling someone you trust them is incredibly powerful. It gives them confidence and the courage to take action.

I put employees first, and I expect them to be happy at work. I have felt trust and love during my personal growth, and I want to bring that to the working environment as well. To achieve this, we are planning creative staff activities to celebrate our past failures in business. I hope this takes the burden down from our employees and inspires more to dare speaking up.

I recently watched a movie about Mother Teresa. Much of her philosophy resonated with me when I thought about my start-up journey. I realized that there was no predefined road map or logical framework to follow. It was a leap of faith, a willingness to venture into the unknown.

Mother Teresa once likened herself to being a mere instrument in the hands of God. Her statement, though I can't recall the exact phrasing, conveyed the idea that she saw herself as a channel—a pencil—through which divine purpose and guidance flowed. It wasn't about her personal desires or ambitions; rather, she believed that she was entrusted with a sacred mission. She listened to God's voice and followed what she believed was His directive with unwavering persistence.

We can connect our hearts with the universe, allowing it to guide our actions. Mother Teresa's example serves as a reminder of how one can become an instrument of higher forces, transcending personal limitations and embracing a profound sense of purpose.

Reflection exercise

- Which moments of your day bring you closer to your inner self and the message of your heart?
- What holds you back?
- How might you change that?

Next

Like most people, my focus when I started was on success. Then, I realized there is more than one way to succeed.

CHAPTER 7

Wolf and Water

Alone we can do so little; together we can do so much.

—Helen Keller

I want to share with you two concepts here, one of wolf and one of water. I share them because I suspect that perhaps you believe, as I once did, that succeeding in business and caring for people are conflicting values, but I can assure you that they can coexist.

Let's look at an imaginary scenario. Suppose Entrepreneur A opens a gas station on a corner. Pretty soon, Entrepreneur B says, "I'm going to build a bigger gas station and destroy Entrepreneur A." So, that gas station is the wolf that devours the first gas station. However, the way of the wolf is not one of peaceful coexistence, and soon Entrepreneurs C, D, and E—each one larger than the other—systematically move in and destroy the other. Well, you might think, that's the way of business. The largest wolf wins; however, the largest wolf will be the corporation that moves in and devours the last-standing entrepreneur. Even if you're the largest now, you will share the same destination as others before you. It's all a matter of time.

The wolf's approach to business enforces a single winner. In this paradigm, for there to be a winner, everyone else must lose, regardless of the circumstances. This demonstrates the essence of the wolf theory. This business approach resembles zero-sum thinking, encapsulated by the notion of "Your gain is my loss," or, conversely, "Your loss is my gain." In other words, one must suffer for the other to thrive. However, in real life, there's often a more sustainable solution.

What if we did it differently? Entrepreneur A opens a gas station on a corner. The business does well, and Entrepreneur B decides, "This looks like a successful corner. I'm going to build a coffee shop next door." Then, Entrepreneur C, attracted to the thriving location, opens a grocery store. The area becomes an ecosystem, everyone with a different goal with no need to compete. With multidimensional measurements, we create a more open market or world that allows everyone to thrive.

The way of the wolf is about destruction. It is about bigger and better with no end in sight. Yet, when most of us enter the business world, the way of the wolf is what we're taught we need to be and to follow in order to survive and thrive. I, certainly, was taught this.

In addition to business success, we need meaning in life. It is vital. If we embrace personal meaning and growth, we can not only achieve but also inspire those around us. In a business setting, this philosophy will move from us to our colleagues, our partners, and our customers.

The way of water

Every company has its unique philosophy. By that, I mean we are not all the same; we are multilayered and full of life at every level. Culture is about finding a suitable approach to accommodate the needs of many people. It is not about enforcing uniformity.

In the not-so-distant past, we believed that only wolf-like companies could succeed. Ruthlessness, both external and internal, prevailed. Yet, there are companies—mine included—that do succeed despite their different philosophies. For us, water embodies qualities we admire, such as perseverance and nurturing. When you nurture others, you are also nourishing yourself—we prosper together or decline together.

Water also has a quiet power. Constant dripping can wear away stone. So, the way of water is not about weakness.

Being quiet and soft doesn't equate to being weak. I remember reading an old Chinese story a long time ago about our tongue and teeth—they coexist in the mouth. While it may seem that teeth dominate the competition for space because of their hardness, occasionally even causing discomfort to the tongue, that doesn't imply that the tongue is weaker or more useless than the hard teeth. In the long run, when we've lost all our teeth with age, the tongue remains in the mouth, faithfully performing its function as it has for years. Soft doesn't mean weak; it's not hard, yet it endures.

And creating a caring company is not about weakness. Ultimately, we are social animals; we need one another. We must value connection more than attacking and conquering. That connection is what our company values and what it lives by. As I write this book, we are launching a series of offline and online workshops and various Inner Mountain community activities in both the United States and

China. I'm excited to see the direction this will take us and those who accompany us on the journey.

For us, embodying the essence of water goes beyond mere philosophy or theory; it's a daily practice ingrained in our behavior and conduct. This belief shapes our demeanor at DHgate, guiding our approach to business in every new country or locale we venture into. Our focus is on seamlessly integrating into the local environment, particularly adapting ourselves to the needs of small businesses. We keenly observe their challenges, identify opportunities for synergy, and assist them in establishing and growing their enterprises.

Unlike the conventional approach of competing aggressively or challenging local businesses as outsiders, in every market, we operate by adhering to the principles of the water theory—maintaining a quietly brilliant and soft presence, refraining from biting or harming others for our survival. This approach has garnered us acceptance and appreciation. We prioritize serving local small and medium-sized businesses rather than engaging in direct competition with the local community.

Despite the evolving business landscape, our unwavering commitment remains steadfast: standing behind micro, small, and medium-sized businesses and individual entrepreneurs. Whether a retailer commenced operations offline, ventured into online retail on platforms like DHgate, or embraced the current trend of social commerce, the core of our support remains constant. The transition from offline to online to social may be dynamic, but our consistent role is to empower MSMEs and provide services, ensuring their success. Thus, our business model is rooted in this enduring philosophy, emphasizing practical implementation rather than mere instruction.

What do you value?

The way of the wolf values only one thing: success. However, that's a pretty limited view, and we know where it ends. Organizations need both material and spiritual aspects to thrive. As important as focusing on making a living is, it should not be the sole purpose. Focusing on it alone will lead to an endless pursuit without inner peace. Comparing yourself to others and feeling good about their failures won't take you far. The initial rush might be there, but the ultimate satisfaction will not be.

Seek meaning in life and strive for personal and collective happiness. Nurturing others and achieving mutual success underscore building relationships, sharing successes, and cultivating a supportive environment. They align with the concept that contributing to the success of others ultimately boosts our own. While we strive to succeed, we don't react fiercely when others succeed first. Instead, we enthusiastically support and nurture others, seeking a win-win success where everyone stands together in the end.

Supporting and nurturing fellow individuals or businesses is not a threat but a pathway to collective prosperity. It's about fostering an environment where everyone has the opportunity to thrive, creating a win-win scenario that goes beyond individual achievements.

This is the vision of the Inner Mountain Foundation:

We envision a world of empowered women who lead, nurture, and inspire those around them—starting with themselves—through the strength they uncover within after climbing and discovering their Inner Mountains.

THE VALUES OF THE INNER MOUNTAIN FOUNDATION

- Spiritual and Material Harmony

- Power from Within

- Confidence from the Climb

- Success Is in the Self

- Sustainability through Community

- Inspiration through Education

- Global Change through Individual Empowerment

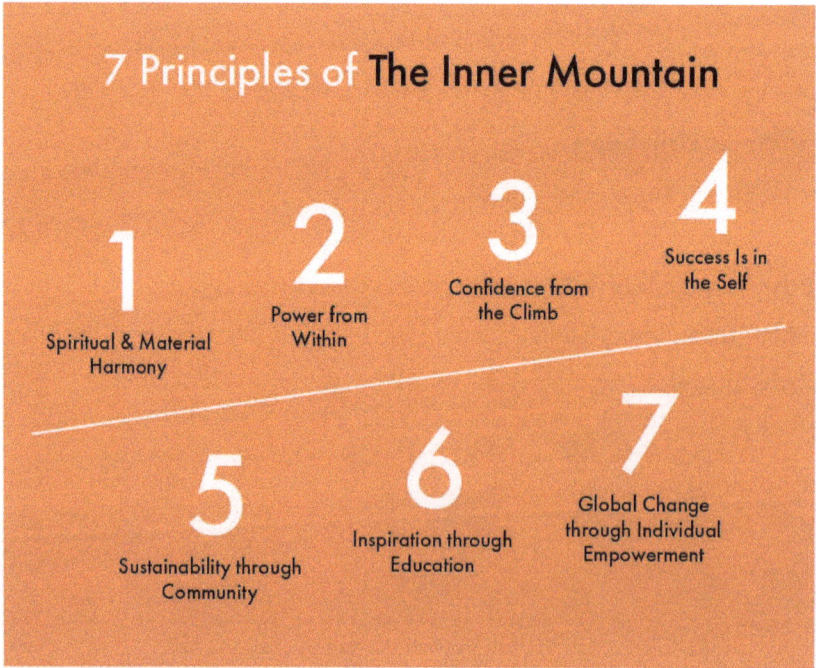

7 Principles of **The Inner Mountain**

1 Spiritual & Material Harmony

2 Power from Within

3 Confidence from the Climb

4 Success Is in the Self

5 Sustainability through Community

6 Inspiration through Education

7 Global Change through Individual Empowerment

Reflection exercise

Think about what experiences in your life and career aligned to the way of the wolf. Do you see this as sustainable? What did you gain from these experiences? What did you lose?

How would you like to approach the next chapter of your life? What would you like to leave behind? What would you like to take with you?

What's next

The future is next. I'm excited to share with you my thoughts about what lies ahead.

CHAPTER 8

Looking to the Future

Don't wait until you're thirsty to dig a well.

—Zhu Xi

Where does true entrepreneurship begin? It's not a job you apply for in the usual way; you won't find a listing for it online. Like much of what we've been exploring in this book, it starts within. It usually appears as a concept, and that concept starts with a dream. As we've already discussed, the first mountain takes you and that dream to reality, to the ups and downs of success, while you climb ever higher. Then, you may pause and look around at your world.

I compare it to astronauts who want to go to the moon. That is their first mountain. Then, when they achieve that, and they look back, they see the world. That amazing moment changes them. And when we are that profoundly changed, we are not the same person anymore. What strikes me especially about this is that the astronaut initially had his heart set on landing on the moon. This goal is similar to how we might focus on the first mountain in our career. His mindset was on the first mountain. Then, he discovers the second mountain, and everything changes—including perspective. Sometimes, looking back is the best way to see. Beautiful Earth was right there all along, but he never realized it. In a way, that's what happened to me when I discovered my inner mountain. I looked back at where I had been and what I had done, and I discovered a new world within myself.

As I finish writing this book, my team and I are engaged in developing pilot programs for the Inner Mountain community members, including the offline and online workshops mentioned in the previous chapter. These programs are one component of our comprehensive system of operations, which include a volunteer pool and focus groups.

IMF Chinese Chapter event

In China, we have focus groups that target a broad range of female entrepreneurs in the cross-border e-commerce sector, as well as those in the international business sphere. This includes not only small and medium-size enterprises but also female entrepreneurs in the wider international business community.

The initial intention behind selecting this group is our ability to gain profound insights. We can discuss and extend ideas freely.

Tears sometimes flow. Emotions are genuine. In the past, I have participated in online courses and industry events, but I have never encountered such a warm and supportive community. Here, members can touch upon emotions they have never before had an opportunity, occasion, or outlet to express. While navigating the entrepreneurial journey, they also carry societal expectations. If everything goes well, that's great. However, when family issues arise, their primary concern is to care for their families. Thus, members face not only work-related pressures but also the anxieties of personal life and child-rearing. Some women have encountered bottlenecks in their careers, unable to break through for many years. They ponder how to transcend their own limitations within organizations and as leaders.

Within our community, many volunteers contribute selflessly with love, dedicating themselves to caring for one another. The community encompasses skills and business knowledge and also integrates individual life situations, providing companionship and compassion. Regardless of what issues arise, members can share within this group. Further, we have a cohort of experienced and compassionate individuals willing to assist them in overcoming challenges, regardless of the source.

In the business realm, practical skills and training can nurture interests. Even more crucial is building upon a solid foundation within ourselves. We can learn skills anytime, anywhere, but breaking through internal barriers, surpassing limitations, having the courage to stand up, and freely expressing ourselves are more crucial. These fundamental constraints might include doubting your own abilities or feeling uncomfortable about drawing attention to yourself. In reality, if these limitations can be overcome, skills will no longer be an issue. As I've said from the first pages of this book, the most difficult limitations are internal. Once you resolve them, the others begin to shrink.

In our pursuit of the first mountain of success, we often focus more on external perspectives, looking outward. Society's standards and requirements seldom lead us to look inward, resulting in a lack of willingness and methods to delve deeply into ourselves. This is the concept of the inner mountain, which we've designed to showcase transformations and discoveries at the foundational level and their connections with the external world. I'm proud to say this is what sets our community apart. Through the acquisition of skills, we can attain a dual peak state, where we simultaneously look inward and outward. This will help us break free from the limitations at the fundamental level on the aspect of "being."

I see our flexible structure as five steps:
- evolving
- closing the loop
- scaling
- feeling your inner power
- giving back

No one makes you do this, and the process may not be the same for you as it is for someone else. In fact, it probably won't be, because this is about personal evolution. Steps one, two, three, and four are for success. Step four occurs after you can truly feel your inner power.

That leads you to step five. You'll want to—indeed you may be driven to—give back.

Evolving takes as long as it takes. A closed loop is a cycle that keeps turning. After the closed loop, there's scale. This isn't difficult for us because our expertise lies in building platforms, and our business model incorporates many such designs. Throughout our journey of entrepreneurship and business management, we have acquired the knowledge of how to construct sustainable business models and create mechanisms that facilitate continuous growth. As we establish and operate this platform, we aim to apply this experience to serve the community. We not only have a clear vision, but we also understand how to design a mechanism that ensures sustainable growth and benefits a larger audience.

In short, we operate DHgate and MyyShop as a platform, so our capabilities are certainly different from those of typical charitable organizations. We aim to leverage our expertise to develop a sustainable mechanism and enable nonprofit organizations, foundations, and social enterprises to scale and assist more people. To put it sentimentally, even if I am not here, this organization should continue to operate sustainably.

One chapter of Inner Mountain is in China, and one is in the United States. In the future, we envision expanding to more emerging or underdeveloped markets, to help more people in need. The community will follow in the footsteps of DHgate, our new site, and MyyShop. With these footsteps, Inner Mountain can reach more places. People need to be connected in communities, and while our society has many mechanisms that serve self-centeredness and individualism—what I call the way of the wolf—we need more. We need a sense of belonging, connection, safety, and love, fundamental human needs that can be fulfilled through a community. Without a framework and a mechanism, these are just empty words, so we are talking less and doing more—designing a mechanism that is valuable and meaningful.

It's an exciting time for us and for me. After the podcast series and digital courses for Inner Mountain members, we foresee more kinds of materials to empower and to communicate in the future.

Once you're successful, you bring others along. That's why I wrote this book; that's why I hope you take the thoughts I share with you here into your own life and your own community. There is another way to look at and live life. I challenge you to discover *your* inner mountain. Because in seeing yourself, you are also able to enlighten others too. That is a sustainable way forward for you and for our fragile, beautiful world.

CONTACT IMF

The Inner Mountain Foundation is a global community empowering women to stand up, speak out, and make a difference, starting with the first step of doing the work within, to overcome the limiting beliefs that hold us back from becoming the best version of ourselves possible.

Join The Inner Mountain Foundation for a journey of inner discovery and growth. Visit innermountain.org to learn more.

ACKNOWLEDGMENTS

I extend my heartfelt gratitude to the incredible individuals and organizations who have played a significant role in shaping this book and my entrepreneurial journey.

First and foremost, I want to express my appreciation to the dedicated teams involved in the creation of this book. Your hard work and commitment have been invaluable.

A profound thank you to the colleagues who have been steadfast companions throughout my entrepreneurial process. The journey wouldn't have been the same without your collective efforts. While the list is extensive, each one of you holds a special place in my heart.

I would like to acknowledge the connections I've forged with APEC organizations and the impactful colleagues from international organizations, especially those involved in programs like APEC CBET and APEC Women Connect. Your collaboration has been instrumental in the development of meaningful initiatives.

Special recognition goes to the China Head at Microsoft and Cisco Jia-bin Duh, and Xiaomi Corporation's Founder, Chairman, and CEO Jun Lei, who served as pillars of support at the start of my leadership journey.

A heartfelt thank you to the investors who believed in the vision and contributed to the journey's success, with special mention of Tina Ju and Hai-Yan Wu for their invaluable support.

My sincere appreciation to my past teachers Zhi-Qiang He from high school, Jie Tang and Bo Shao, whose inspirations and resources have been crucial in navigating the uncharted territories of the inner world.

I'd like to express my gratitude to Bonnie Hearn Hill for her incredible contributions to this book. Bonnie's unique perspective and insightful discussions were essential to its creation. Thank you, Bonnie, for your support and inspiration throughout this journey.

Finally, I cannot overlook the profound influence of my family, my husband Jun Shen, my parents, Xing-Ren Wang and Jing-Ting Yang, my parents-in-law, Zu-Pei Shen and Yu-Ying Song, my sister and brother, Shu-Ling Wang & Shu-Ping Wang, and my kids, Yu-He Shen and Xue-Hua Shen, whose unwavering support has been my anchor throughout this entrepreneurial venture.

To everyone who has been a part of this incredible journey, thank you for your contributions, encouragement, and belief in the vision. This book is a reflection of our collective efforts and shared experiences.

ABOUT THE AUTHOR

Diane Wang is the founder, chairperson, and CEO at DHGATE Group, one of China's leading cross-border B2B e-commerce marketplaces, founded in 2004. Diane's journey is one of passion, determination, and immense contribution to women's empowerment. Through her leadership, she has inspired countless women to pursue their dreams and achieve greatness.

Diane is passionate about driving the digital inclusion agenda for MSMEs (Micro, Small, & Medium Enterprises) and women, collaborating with international associations and agencies.

WTO Director General's Business Advisory Group Member

B20 Women in Business Action Council, Co-Chair

B20 MSME & Entrepreneurship Working Group, Co-Chair

B20 Digital Transformation Task Force, Co-Chair

APEC Business Advisory Council (ABAC), Member

ABAC Women's Forum, Chair

World Internet Conference Organizing Committee, High-Level Advisory Council Member

TEDx Speaker

www.ingramcontent.com/pod-product-compliance
Lightning Source LLC
Chambersburg PA
CBHW040223110426
42813CB00036B/3461/J